# The Church Of God In Christ Presiding Bishop

Bishop Charles E. Blake, Sr.

W9-CPE-755

## Christ's Extreme Sacrifice Calls For Our Extreme Commitment

*"For the love of Christ constraineth us; because we thus judge, that if one died for all, then were all dead: And that he died for all, that they which live should not henceforth live unto themselves, but unto him which died for them, and rose again."*
*- 2 Corinthians 5:14-15 (KJV)*

Order materials today from the Power for Living Series:

Church Of God In Christ Publishing House
2500 Lamar Avenue, Memphis, Tennessee 38114
P.O. Box 140636, Memphis, Tennessee 38114
Toll Free: 1-877-746-8578 | Fax: (901) 743-1555
Website: www.cogicpublishinghouse.net
Email: sales@cogicpublishinghouse.net

# FROM THE PRESIDING BISHOP'S DESK

To All Diligent Workers and Students of Sunday School,

It is my honor and privilege to address you in these quarterly Sunday School lessons. It is in Sunday School that we learn the Word of God, discuss the lessons for growth and knowledge, and come together as a community within itself. Sunday School is a living, breathing community all on its own within the church; it breathes new life, revelation, and friendships. During this fall quarter, the lessons will take a focus on the Christian Community Coming Alive. These powerful lessons will teach us the importance of praying for one another, the power of sharing our gifts and talents with each other to enhance the Kingdom of God, and most of all, the way we are to bring our communities together.

The tragic events of Ferguson, New York, and Baltimore all show us that we must engage our communities around our local churches, with prayer for hurting families, fasting to break the chains of injustice for all people, and the love and power of the Word of God to show that we are stronger together with God in our daily lives. As the Presiding Bishop of our great church, we must stand together united in love, prayer, fasting, and the compassion of God. It was through God's compassion that we were created, and that He gave us Jesus Christ to save us from our sins, and also that we have been given the Word of God to live by.

Thank you, God bless you, and let us help make the Christian community come alive within our churches and in our surrounding communities. Remember Genesis 11:6: "And the LORD said, Behold, the people is one, and they have all one language: and this they begin to do: and now nothing will be restrained from them, which they have imagined to do" (KJV).

I would like to thank the Church Of God In Christ Publishing Board/Publishing House of the Church Of God In Christ for their continued fine work and dedication to the Saints of God. Thanks to the International Departments who continually keep our literature as their resource curriculum of choice. Thanks so much to this fine team who have shown that they are extremely committed to excellence in the Word of God.

Bishop Charles Edward Blake Sr.
Presiding Bishop
Seventh in Succession
Church Of God In Christ, Inc.

# FROM THE DESK OF CHAIRMAN MARK ELLIS

Greetings to the People of God,

What a blessing it is to know that we have a God on our side who not only looks out for us, but also greets us with love and kindness, and imparts His wisdom in us! Yet, what good does it do for us to not spread that love and kindness among our brothers and sisters? What good does it do for us to withhold that godly wisdom from our friends, families, and more importantly our community?

Jeremiah 31:3 says, "With lovingkindness have I drawn thee," and it is through that same loving kindness that we draw and engage our community. The Christian community has all of the benefits of Heaven. Those benefits which have been given to us by God can afford us the ability to share, communicate, and pass them on, but what good does it do that community if we do not share any of them with others? It's our time to come alive in the Body of Christ! Why? Just as Jesus Christ is yet alive, He requires that same spirit of life to be alive in us. It is that same spirit of liveliness which will determine if we go back with Him when He comes again, and we must bring not only ourselves but our community with us. Our Lord and Savior Jesus Christ is not selfish, and He definitely demands that we must become just like Him.

I encourage every reader to become extremely committed to the Word of God and get into this quarter with excitement and expectation, as we break down the Scriptures.

Thank you so much for believing in the Church Of God In Christ Publishing House. Come and join me in this journey this quarter.

Superintendent Mark A. Ellis
Chairman of the Publishing Board
Church Of God In Christ, Inc.

# FROM THE CHAIRMAN OF MARKETING

To All Students and Workers of Sunday School,

As an attendee of Sunday School, I am excited to address you each and every time in our quarterly lessons. I believe that the Sunday School Department is the prime entity for bringing unity and the knowledge of God to the forefront of our communities. Building up our communities shows that we are diligent workers of Christ, seriously committed to building the Kingdom of God. In this fall quarter, the Lord is showing us little by little that His coming is soon; we must be found working and full of love.

Jesus Christ spoke only a few times in the synagogue, but the majority of His sermons were preached outside of the city to accommodate the people. The only way that we can truly show the love of Christ and the grace of God is by engaging the Christian community and energizing it to come alive in love, power, and authority. To do this, we must come together in prayer for one another—that's the love; we must trust in the Holy Ghost that He is working on our behalf—that's the power; and we must know that the Spirit is "Not for Sale"—that's our authority. When we combine these three things with the Word of God, we cannot help but become unified together under His awesome power.

We, the Church Of God In Christ body, are stronger together, and our communities need us just like we need them. For Jesus Christ is getting us ready for His Second Coming, and what better way to be prepared than by working in our local communities.

Many thanks to the Saints of God, the Church Of God In Christ Publishing Board, and the Publishing House for their continued dedication to the Word and Work of the Lord. Thanks to all of the departments and churches across the country for their loyal support of the Church Of God In Christ's literature. As always, let me personally thank each of you for your continued support and encouragement by purchasing the curriculums. *Remember, without you, this dream wouldn't have become a reality, and a church without its people is just an empty shell.*

Yours for service,

Evangelist Sandra Smith Jones
Chairman of Marketing/Sales, Publishing Board
Church Of God In Christ

# QUARTERLY COMMENTARY

## FALL 2015

### SEPTEMBER · OCTOBER · NOVEMBER

## The Christian Community Comes Alive

### EDITORIAL STAFF:

Superintendant Mark A. Ellis, Chairman
Church Of God In Christ Publishing Board

Charles E. Blake, Sr., Presiding Bishop and Chief Apostle
The Church Of God In Christ, Incorporated

# PRAYING FOR ONE ANOTHER

**BIBLE BASIS:** ACTS 4:23–31

**BIBLE TRUTH:** Prayer is a powerful weapon that God has given His people.

**MEMORY VERSE:** "And when they had prayed, the place was shaken where they were assembled together; and they were all filled with the Holy Ghost, and they spake the word of God with boldness" (Acts 4:31).

**LESSON AIM:** By the end of the lesson, we will: REVIEW the apostles' prayer for strength to speak with boldness and to continue Jesus' ministry while under political duress; GAIN insights into prayer as a means through which Christians can remain strong voices for change and effective ministries in their communities today; and ASK God in bold prayers to empower their mission and ministry.

## LESSON SCRIPTURE

### ACTS 4:23–31, KJV

**23** And being let go, they went to their own company, and reported all that the chief priests and elders had said unto them.

**24** And when they heard that, they lifted up their voice to God with one accord, and said, Lord, thou art God, which hast made heaven, and earth, and the sea, and all that in them is:

**25** Who by the mouth of thy servant David hast said, Why did the heathen rage, and the people imagine vain things?

**26** The kings of the earth stood up, and the rulers were gathered together against the Lord, and against his Christ.

**27** For of a truth against thy holy child Jesus, whom thou hast anointed, both Herod, and Pontius Pilate, with the Gentiles, and the people of Israel, were gathered together,

**28** For to do whatsoever thy hand and thy counsel determined before to be done.

**29** And now, Lord, behold their threatenings: and grant unto thy servants, that with all boldness they may speak thy word,

**30** By stretching forth thine hand to heal; and that signs and wonders may be done by the name of thy holy child Jesus.

**31** And when they had prayed, the place was shaken where they were assembled together; and they were all filled with the Holy Ghost, and they spake the word of God with boldness.

## LIFE NEED FOR TODAY'S LESSON

**AIM: You will discuss how you share your various gifts and talents in various ways.**

## INTRODUCTION

### The Power of God's Word

In Chapter 3, God uses Peter to heal a crippled man who sat at the temple gate daily begging for help. Once the man was healed, he began to dance and praise God to the amazement of those around him. Peter and John used this moment as an opportunity to share the Gospel of Jesus Christ and explain how faith in Christ made the man whole. The priests, temple guard, and Sadducees were disturbed by Peter and John teaching the people about

Jesus and His Resurrection, and threw them both in jail. As a result of Peter and John's message, the church added five thousand believers. The council was afraid of the people's reaction if they were to harm Peter and John, so they decided to bring them before the council and question them.

The Holy Spirit gave Peter the courage to speak and the words to say to the council. The council was amazed by the boldness and skillful use of Scripture by these ordinary men. Since they were not able to deny the miracle that had been performed, the council decided to try to stop the Gospel's spread by demanding that Peter and John stop preaching about Jesus and threatening them.

## BIBLE LEARNING

**AIM: You will learn that the Holy Spirit will fill you to speak God's Word with boldness.**

## I. PREPARED FOR OPPOSITION (Acts 4:23)

In **verse 23**, Peter and John return to the believers and share all that the council did and said to them. Jesus had warned His followers of this very situation (**Luke 12:11–12**). Peter and John had experienced opposition because of their commitment to the Gospel. They had healed a crippled beggar in the name of Jesus. This had confused the council members of the Sanhedrin because Peter and John were not religious teachers, but men of Galilee who healed in the name of Jesus of Nazareth, a man the council had condemned to death.

Peter and John reported to the fledgling church what the Sanhedrin told them. They were officially told to not speak or preach in the name of Jesus. It wasn't the healing that was so bad in the eyes of the Jewish leaders, but the Gospel message and the name of Jesus.

The two apostles were beaten as an act of discipline to ensure the Sanhedrin's orders were followed. This beating was also probably used as an example to instill fear in their followers. Ultimately Peter and John rejoiced in their suffering, since they were suffering for Christ. It was the treasure of the Gospel message that inspired the prayers of the new church, and it should inspire our prayers as well.

## Acts 4:23–31

**23 And being let go, they went to their own company, and reported all that the chief priests and elders had said unto them.**

The expression "their own company" (Gk. *idios*, **I-dee-os**), or "their own circle," denotes the Christian community. It suggests that after their release, Peter and John returned to "headquarters," perhaps the Upper Room of **Acts 1:13**, where members of the new community had no doubt been engaged in intercessory prayer for them. They reported their experience with the council. This report must have caused the early company fear. The persecution of leaders is a tactic that is often used to silence their followers.

## II. GOD PREVAILS OVER OPPOSITION (vv. 24–28)

This portion of the lesson begins what is sometimes called the Believer's Prayer. These early believers quote **Psalm 2** in their prayer. This psalm, most likely a coronation psalm, is attributed to David. It describes the hostility that accompanied the installation of a king. The king, God's servant, is a consecrated worshiper and the recipient of hostility from the Gentile nations. As the nations attempt to oppose or dethrone the king God has anointed, they are told it is all for nothing; their efforts will fail. These nations are not just opposing an earthly king, but God Himself.

The believers go on to describe the hostility that Jesus faced at the hands of these same leaders and how their treatment of Jesus did not derail God's divine plan. The Jewish leaders and Roman authorities had attempted to silence Jesus in death, but in vain—He rose from the dead. Now Jesus is crowned Lord of the universe due to His Resurrection and ascension to Heaven. The believers trust in the resurrected King who is sovereign over the authorities of this earth. Any attempt at opposing the spread of the Gospel message is a vain attempt. Just like the Gentile kings of **Psalm 2**, the Jewish leaders' opposition is in vain.

**24 And when they heard that, they lifted up their voice to God with one accord, and said, Lord, thou art God, which hast made heaven, and earth, and the sea, and all that in them is.**

With one accord, they turned to God in prayer. The Greek word for "one accord" or "together" is *homothumadon* (**ho-mo-thoo-ma-DON**), which indicates that they were like one person in prayer. It is a combination of two Greek words meaning "together" and "passion." The disciples were all praying together with the same passion and ardor. It does not mean they all simultaneously said the same words. One of the leaders may have prayed accompanied by a responsive "amen" from the rest. It was more like an orchestra with the Holy Spirit as the conductor. There is power in a gathering of believers when they are in "one accord" (see **vv. 24–31**).

They addressed God as "Lord" or "Master" (Gk. *despotes*, **des-POE-tace**), a term denoting the sovereignty of God and His absolute control over all creation. The term is also used for a slave owner or a ruler with unchallengeable

power. In the disciples' prayer, the term certainly points to the fact that the authority of the council was subject to a higher authority still, and that the law of men cannot overturn the decrees of God (cf. **vv. 19–20**). The disciples filled their minds with thoughts of the sovereignty of God before stating their petition. The sovereign God is the God of creation. He made the heaven, the earth, the sea, and everything in them (cf. **17:24, 26**; see also **Nehemiah 9:6; Psalm 146:6**).

**25 Who by the mouth of thy servant David hast said, Why did the heathen rage, and the people imagine vain things? 26 The kings of the earth stood up, and the rulers were gathered together against the Lord, and against his Christ. 27 For of a truth against thy holy child Jesus, whom thou hast anointed, both Herod, and Pontius Pilate, with the Gentiles, and the people of Israel, were gathered together. 28 For to do whatsoever thy hand and thy counsel determined before to be done.**

The sovereign Lord is the God of revelation. He had revealed to His servant David the opposition Christ would face from various groups. "Why did the heathen rage" is quoted from **Psalm 2:1–2**. **Psalm 2** originally referred to the accession of a Davidic king, the Lord's Anointed, and the revolt of His vassals. It was interpreted by the Jews and the early Christian church as a Messianic psalm (cf. **Acts 13:33; Hebrews 5:5**). In the psalm, the "heathen" (Gk. **ETH-nos**, people other than the Israelites) is paired with the "people" (Gk. **lah-OSE**, Israelites, the people of God). In other words, both God's people and those from outside resisted God's chosen leader. Here the community references the psalm to reveal the extent of Jesus' rejection as the Messiah. Once again, it is only a few from among God's people and from the Gentiles who accept God's chosen Messiah.

"The kings of the earth" (and "the rulers", who stood up against the Lord and His Christ, were represented by Herod Antipas, the Tetrarch of Galilee and Peraea (**Luke 23:7**), Pontius Pilate, and even Herod the Great, who attempted to kill Jesus at the start of His time on earth. This shows that the sovereign Lord is the God of history. The Greek conjunction *gar* (**GAR**), which indicates a cause or reason proves the truth of the preceding prophecy by pointing to its historical fulfillment. Herod, Pontius Pilate, the Gentiles, and the people of Israel are clearly identified with the kings, the rulers, the nations, and the people of **Psalm 2:1–2** as quoted in **Acts 4:25**.

The expression "thy holy child Jesus" explicitly identifies Jesus with the royal Son of God addressed in **Psalm 2:7**. Jesus is both the obedient Son and the One whom God anointed or made Messiah. Jesus, "whom thou hast anointed," refers to the Holy Spirit's identification of Him as Messiah at His baptism. The Holy Spirit's resting on Jesus signaled His anointing or empowerment and the inauguration of His earthly ministry (cf. **10:38; Luke 3:21–22; 4:18–21; Isaiah 61:1**).

## SEARCH THE SCRIPTURES

### QUESTION 1
The Holy Spirit gave Peter the ability to do what?

### QUESTION 2
Who are the "kings of the earth"?

## III. EMPOWERED FOR OPPOSITION (vv. 29–31)

At the end of the prayer, the believers appeal to God to give them greater boldness and empower them to perform greater works in Jesus' name. They accept and embrace the fact that they will face opposition. David faced it. Jesus faced it. Their request is not for God to alleviate it or make a way for them to escape it. They are not concerned about themselves, but focused on the Gospel being heard, and they understand that the plan of God has a history of hostility from those who feel threatened by it. They seek God and ask to be empowered and strengthened so that they can continue to serve Him with boldness.

God responds to their request with a physical sign: the entire place shakes. This must have confirmed and strengthened their faith. The disciples are then empowered with boldness to preach the name of Jesus. It is important to note that the power the apostles sought was so they could better serve God and others, while the power that the council sought was strictly for their own benefit. As we seek God for power, we need to have a proper understanding of what power is for. God empowers us to serve others and not ourselves.

29 And now, Lord, behold their threatenings: and grant unto thy servants, that will all boldness they may speak thy word. 30 By stretching forth thine hand to heal; and that signs and wonders may be done by the name of thy holy child Jesus. 31 And when they had prayed, the place of shaken where they assembled together; and they were all filled with the Holy Ghost, and they spake the word of God with boldness.

The council's threats were not a cause for fear and silence, but bolder speech. The apostles therefore prayed that they might have courage to proclaim the Word of God "with all boldness." The Greek word for "boldness" (*parresia*, **pah-reh-SEE-a**) in this context refers to freedom in speaking and unreservedness of utterance. The disciples wanted to speak the message of the Gospel without fear. The word "servants" comes from the Greek word *doulos* (**DOO-las**), which means slave and contrasts with the majesty of "Lord" from **verse 24**.

The disciples' next request is that God would place the seal of His public approval on their witness by granting further mighty works of healing and similar signs and wonders through the same name that had cured the lame man—the name of Jesus.

The term "hand," most frequently used to refer to God's act of punishment, here denotes His action in bringing blessing (cf. **Luke 5:13**). It was of course the apostles' hands that were stretched out to heal, but, as in **Acts 3:16**, they attributed their power to God working through them as they restored men to wholeness in the name of Jesus.

The account here is reminiscent of the description of what happened on the Day of Pentecost, both in the external signs of the Spirit's coming and in the disciples' prayerful attitude when He comes. In answer to the disciples' united and earnest prayers, the place was shaken, they were all filled with the Holy Spirit, and they proclaimed the Word of God boldly. They were encouraged to continue to proclaim the faith despite the council's threats.

The shaking (Gk. *saleuo*, **sal-EW-oh**) of the place where the disciples were symbolizes the presence of God (cf. **Exodus 19:18; Isaiah 6:4**). The assurance of divine favor and help came even as they prayed. An earthquake might be a cause for fear to some, but to those who see it as an answer to prayer, it is an encouragement. The verb "filled" followed by the verb "spake" indicates the immediate and continuous action of the disciples. They were continuously proclaiming the Word of God with boldness.

## SEARCH THE SCRIPTURES

### QUESTION 3
In **verse 24**, what is the Greek word for boldness, and define what it means in this context.

## BIBLE APPLICATION

**AIM: You will learn that followers of Christ will draw strength from Him as they seek God in prayer.**

Many circumstances in life can challenge our faith and hinder our relationship with God. This is why we must stay ready and willing to pray for one another. In order for Christians to witness boldly, we must have uncompromising trust in God's plan in spite of opposition.

## STUDENT'S RESPONSES

**AIM: Believers will take comfort in knowing that God answers prayer.**

Our ability to effect change is directly related to our prayer life, personal worship, and relationship with God. This is where we start. The church in Acts began with prayer, but their prayer empowered them to go out into the community and do works for the benefit of others. Brainstorm some areas in which your community needs change. Pray as a class for God to empower you to serve. Ask God for boldness to step out and serve the community and watch Him move.

## PRAYER

Dear Lord, we pray for boldness to speak Your Word and live Your Word as we share the Christian faith with others. In the Name of Jesus we pray. Amen.

## HOW TO SAY IT

Sanhedrin.     san-**HEED**-rin.

Sadducees.     sa-dyu-**SEES**.

## PREPARE FOR NEXT SUNDAY

Read **Acts 4:34–5:10** and "Sharing All Things."

### DAILY HOME BIBLE READINGS

**MONDAY**
Prayer of Humility
(Matthew 6:9–15)

**TUESDAY**
Prayer of Gratitude
(2 Chronicles 6:1–15)

**WEDNESDAY**
Open-Hearted Life
(2 Corinthians 6:1–13)

**THURSDAY**
Greater Things Through Prayer
(John 14:11–13)

**FRIDAY**
No One Else
(Acts 4:1–12)

**SATURDAY**
No Other Authority
(Acts 4:13–22)

**SUNDAY**
Praying With Boldness
(Acts 4:23–31)

**Sources:**
Carson, D.A., France, R.T., Motyer, J.A., Wenham, J.G. *New Bible Commentary.* Downers Grove, IL: InterVarsity Press, 1993.
Keener, Craig S. *IVP Bible Background Commentary.* Downers Grove, IL: InterVarsity Press, 1993.
Polhill, John B. Acts. *New American Commentary: An Exegetical and Theological Exposition of Holy Scripture.* Nashville: B&H Publishing, 1992.

## COMMENTS / NOTES:

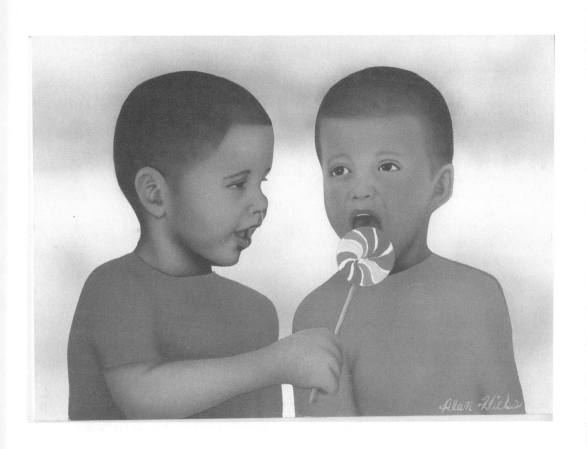

# SHARING ALL THINGS

**BIBLE BASIS:** ACTS 4:34–5:10

**BIBLE TRUTH:** The early followers of Jesus shared everything with one another, so there was not a needy person among them.

**MEMORY VERSE:** "Neither was there any among them that lacked: for as many as were possessors of lands or houses sold them, and brought the prices of the things that were sold" (Acts 4:34).

**LESSON AIM:** By the end of the lesson, we will: UNDERSTAND the sacrifices and rewards of the early Christians' willingness to share their possessions with others; EXAMINE our motivation for making sacrificial offerings; and DRAFT a list of statements that would motivate others to contribute freely to a community project.

## LESSON SCRIPTURE

### ACTS 4:34–5:10, KJV

**34** Neither was there any among them that lacked: for as many as were possessors of lands or houses sold them, and brought the prices of the things that were sold,

**35** And laid them down at the apostles' feet: and distribution was made unto every man according as he had need.

**36** And Joses, who by the apostles was surnamed Barnabas, (which is, being interpreted, The son of consolation,) a Levite, and of the country of Cyprus,

**37** Having land, sold it, and brought the money, and laid it at the apostles' feet.

**5:1** But a certain man named Ananias, with Sapphira his wife, sold a possession,

**2** And kept back part of the price, his wife also being privy to it, and brought a certain part, and laid it at the apostles' feet.

**3** But Peter said, Ananias, why hath Satan filled thine heart to lie to the Holy Ghost, and to keep back part of the price of the land?

**4** Whiles it remained, was it not thine own? and after it was sold, was it not in thine own power? why hast thou conceived this thing in thine heart? thou hast not lied unto men, but unto God.

**5** And Ananias hearing these words fell down, and gave up the ghost: and great fear came on all them that heard these things.

**6** And the young men arose, wound him up, and carried him out, and buried him.

**7** And it was about the space of three hours after, when his wife, not knowing what was done, came in.

**8** And Peter answered unto her, Tell me whether ye sold the land for so much? And she said, Yea, for so much.

**9** Then Peter said unto her, How is it that ye have agreed together to tempt the Spirit of the Lord? behold, the feet of them which have buried thy husband are at the door, and shall carry thee out.

**10** Then fell she down straightway at his feet, and yielded up the ghost: and the young men came in, and found her dead, and, carrying her forth, buried her by her husband.

## LIFE NEED FOR TODAY'S LESSON

AIM: You will appreciate that although there are exceptions, most people are glad to share what they have with those in need.

## INTRODUCTION

### The Spirit of Generosity

The generosity described in this lesson is a continuation of the giving described in Acts 2:44–45: "And all that believed were together, and had all things common; and sold their possessions and goods, and parted them to all men, as every man had need." The Gospel message of Jesus' extravagant love had a significant impact on the early church. The reality of Jesus' tremendous sacrifice inspired them to sacrifice for the benefit of others. They were not comfortable seeing their brothers and sisters in Christ go without. This conviction led them to do more than just pray for their brothers and sisters; it prompted them to take personal action. In this lesson, we see that the spirit of generosity is still needed in the church.

## BIBLE LEARNING

AIM: You will learn that some believers in the early church did not share with those in need and were punished.

## I. UNRESERVED GENEROSITY
## (Acts 4:34–37)

In the Old Testament, we see that God is consistently concerned with the plight of those less fortunate. Israel was chastised many times because they had failed to take care of those unable to take care of themselves: widows, orphans, and the poor. God makes clear that Israel is responsible for taking care of one another (**Deuteronomy 15:4**). He also commands Israel to bring all the

tithes and offerings to the house of God so that there would be provision there (**Malachi 3:10**). This was so the poor would know that they could come to the Temple and find food.

As a response to the generosity Jesus showed them, the early church provided for all so that no one "lacked." Their possessions and goods were shared in common and given to anyone who was in need. This was remarkable in first century Palestine, as most of the population lived in poverty. The early church provided the context to live out Jesus' command to "sell your possessions and give to the poor" (**Matthew 19:21, Luke 12:33, NIV**). The community of the new covenant shared everything.

## Acts 4:35–5:10

34 Neither was there any among them that lacked: for as many as were possessors of lands or houses sold them, and brought the prices of the things that were sold, 35 And laid them down at the apostles' feet: and distribution was made unto every man according as he had need. 36 And Joses, who by the apostles was surnamed Barnabas, (which is, being interpreted, The son of consolation,) a Levite, and of the country of Cyprus, 37 Having land, sold it, and brought the money, and laid it at the apostles' feet.

The first phrase in this verse echoes the words of **Deuteronomy 15:4**: "There shall be no poor among you." In this way, Luke (who wrote Acts to follow his Gospel) paints a picture of the early church as a new Israel. This would have appealed to those in the Jewish community, as they could see the church fulfilling the role of the ideal community in the age to come. This community was attractive to those Jews living in poverty at this time.

What is striking about the Christians' sharing all their goods in common is that it was a voluntary practice. The iterative imperfect tense is used in

**34b–35.** This tense indicates that the community members used to sell their property and share the wealth as a regular practice. There is evidence that the Qumran communities near the Dead Sea around the time of Christ practiced the surrender of property. There is a similar generosity of spirit and on-going commitment to communal needs here in Acts.

Laying the money at the apostles' feet was an act of submission—not to the apostles as mere men, but to Christ. The twelve represented Christ on earth. The act of the believers laying the money at their feet was symbolic of submitting their wealth to Christ. This was not worship of the apostles but a symbolic statement. The apostles actually turned over the responsibility of distributing the proceeds to the seven deacons once this duty distracted them from their main task of prayer and preaching the Word (**Acts 6:1–7**).

Barnabas' given name was Joses or Joseph. The apostles who spoke Aramaic nicknamed Joses "Barnabas," meaning "son of prophecy," from the Aramaic *bar* meaning "son of" and *nabu* meaning "prophecy." Some have given the nickname a slightly different meaning, translating it as "son of refreshment." Based on his intimate knowledge of the man, Luke translated the Aramaic into Greek as *huios parakleseos*, which is translated variously as "son of consolation/exhortation/encouragement." Parakleseos comes from the same root as the word Jesus used in His promise to send the Holy Spirit: "And I will pray to the Father and He will give you another Comforter [*parakletos*], that He may abide with you forever" (**John 14:16**). Luke uses these exact words to indicate that the Holy Spirit had distinguished Himself in Barnabas. It is interesting to note that the main function of prophecy (from which we get part of the compound of Barnabas' name) is to build up, encourage, and comfort (**1 Corinthians 14:3**). Whenever we see Barnabas in the pages of the New Testament, he is building up, encouraging, and comforting others to be their best for Jesus.

## SEARCH THE SCRIPTURES

### QUESTION 1
What was Barnabas' birth name?

## II. Consequences of Deception (5:1–10)

The story of Ananias and Sapphira is puzzling. The generosity displayed by the early church was completely spontaneous. No one was commanded to sell their property and give the money to the apostles. People chose to do it because it was their heart's desire to make sure their brothers and sisters in Christ were well cared for. The field was Ananias and Sapphira's to do with as they pleased. It would stand to reason that if they decided to give the apostles part of the money and keep part of the money for themselves, that would have been perfectly acceptable.

What prompted them to lie to the apostles? Maybe they wanted to appear generous so they could become leaders in the church. Maybe they wanted to be seen giving a lot of money like the rich people in **Mark 12:41–43**. Whatever their reason, what happened to them serves as a strong reminder that the façade we put up to impress others is not able to stand in the presence of the Holy Spirit. God is a discerner of the heart, thoughts, and intents of people. It is impossible to lie to Him; He knows us and whether what we do is sincere or for show and appearance. God will reward us according to our intentions, so make sure that all that you do is done with a pure heart and not a hidden agenda.

**5:1 But a certain man named Ananias, with Sapphira his wife, sold a possession, 2 And kept back part of the price, his wife also being privy to it, and brought a certain part, and laid it at the apostles' feet. 3 But Peter said, Ananias, why hath Satan filled thine heart to lie to the Holy Ghost, and to keep**

back part of the price of the land? 4 Whiles it remained, was it not thine own? and after it was sold, was it not in thine own power? why hast thou conceived this thing in thine heart? thou hast not lied unto men, but unto God. 5 And Ananias hearing these words fell down, and gave up the ghost: and great fear came on all them that heard these things. 6 And the young men arose, wound him up, and carried him out, and buried him. 7 And it was about the space of three hours after, when his wife, not knowing what was done, came in. 8 And Peter answered unto her, Tell me whether ye sold the land for so much? And she said, Yea, for so much. 9 Then Peter said unto her, How is it that ye have agreed together to tempt the Spirit of the Lord? behold, the feet of them which have buried thy husband are at the door, and shall carry thee out. 10 Then fell she down straightway at his feet, and yielded up the ghost: and the young men came in, and found her dead, and, carrying her forth, buried her by her husband. 11 And great fear came upon the whole church and upon all who heard of these things.

Nothing is known about Ananias and his wife Sapphira outside of their sin. It is a sad reminder that sometimes we may be known for all the bad we have done and not the good. The name Ananias means "one whom God has graciously given" and it stands in stark contrast to the stinginess of his actions in this narrative. His actions also stand in stark contrast to the actions of Barnabas, who gave all of the money from the sale of his land to the church. This was in direct contradiction of the work of faith being done in the hearts of those early believers. They truly believed everything was to be shared by all; apparently Ananias and his wife Sapphira did not.

Sapphira was named as an accomplice in this act of selfishness and dishonesty. The Bible does not say that she actually sold the land or kept back the proceeds. It does say that she had knowledge of what Ananias did. She is guilty because she knowingly went along with it. The word in the King James is "privy" (Gk. *sunorao*, **soon-ah-RAH-oh**). It is a compound verb using the Greek words for "together with" and "to see or know." She was not an innocent party but knew what was going on and considered it in her best interest to keep some of the money as well.

Peter as one of the apostles confronts Ananias. The Holy Spirit revealed Ananias' sin to him. Two things come to mind as we look at Peter's words of confrontation. First he says that Satan, not the Holy Spirit, had filled Ananias' heart. The direct influence of Satan himself prompted Ananias to keep some of the money and lie to the apostles and the rest of the church.

Peter then goes right to the heart of the matter. The land was Ananias' property before it was sold. The money was his when he sold the land. It made no sense to lie to the church. Ultimately Ananias did not lie to the church, but to God. He had broken the trust of the community through his selfish and deceptive act. The word for "kept back" can also mean "to pilfer or embezzle." Once Ananias pledged to give the proceeds to the church, it was the Lord's property; to keep some was embezzlement. His act was a sin not just against the community but against God. The word for "conceived" (Gk. *tithemi*, **TI-thay-mee**) also means "set" or "appointed" and indicates the premeditation on the part of Ananias. This was not a knee-jerk reaction, but a planned scheme to deceive the church.

Immediately Ananias is judged, convicted, and executed. We do not know what caused Ananias' death. One thing we know for sure is that this judgment was God's judgment. Immediately the result is that "great fear came upon all who heard it"—not an ordinary fear but a "great fear." Here we see the effect of Ananias' death and the possible reason for Luke including this incident in the narrative. Luke wanted to show the hand of

God in forming the community and protecting its purity.

For the young men to immediately wrap him up and carry him out without ceremony showed that this was divine judgment. In first century Palestine, only the burials of criminals and those who committed suicide were done with this much urgency. The young men were back within a matter of three hours.

Next, Peter confronts Sapphira. She had walked in not knowing what had happened. Luke does not state where this meeting took place and who was present. All he wants the reader to focus on is the seriousness of the couple's deception. Peter questions her on the price of the sale. It doesn't state how much it was and whether it was for good reason—any amount was enough to warrant the judgment of the Lord. Peter in his question gives Sapphira a chance to repent of her wrongdoing. To her demise, she does not repent but continues with the lie.

Peter's reaction is similar to what he said to Ananias: It was not to men that she had lied, but to God. Ananias and Sapphira had both agreed (Gk. *sumphoneo*, **sum-foe-NEH-oh**), which literally means to "sound together" indicating they both were on one accord, indicating their planning to lie to the community. This was not a mere reaction, but a formulated, well thought out plan to deceive the community. Peter then lets Sapphira know she will meet the same fate as her husband.

Sapphira fell down dead in the same way her husband did. The same young men who had carried Ananias out to be buried also carried her out. They were together in their sin, and now they lay together in death. It is interesting to note that Luke mentions the sin and fate of Sapphira as well as her husband. Throughout the books of Luke and Acts, women are given an equal amount of attention as men. It is the same in this case, although Sapphira's actions are far from praiseworthy. Still, it shows Luke's focus on the value of women as equal agents and recipients in God's economy.

Again we hear that "a great fear" comes on not only the whole church, but also everyone who heard about these things. Here we see Luke writing not only from a spiritual perspective, but also as an apologist for the church. He is showing his audience that the early church community was the real thing. It was in fact God's community empowered by the Spirit and tasked to continue the ministry of the crucified and resurrected Messiah.

## SEARCH THE SCRIPTURES

### QUESTION 2

Was Ananias free to do what he wanted to do with the money after selling his land?

## BIBLE APPLICATION

**AIM: You will learn that believers in Christ are responsible to care for others.**

Today it seems like people are quick to cast the church and Christians in a negative light. Pastors of large congregations are criticized for their congregations being too large. Pastors of small congregations are criticized for their congregations not growing. This is all the more reason for us to make sure that we are sincere in all that we do. Engaging in pointless arguments will not do anything to advance the cause of Christianity. However, displays of sincere compassion, generosity, and concern will silence any critic.

## STUDENT'S RESPONSES

**AIM: You will understand that believers should have the right intentions when caring for those in need.**

We at times get stuck thinking that making periodic contributions to the "Benevolence Fund" is all that we need to do in terms of helping others. While making contributions is a great thing, this lesson emphasizes the whole community's responsibility to care for all those in need. Together with the class, plan a project in which you can pool your resources together to sacrificially help someone in need.

## PRAYER

Dear Jesus, help us to be honest with You, ourselves, and others. Let us not create stories and lies that cause pain, problems, and even death. As we accept the purity of Your love and goodness, we will create hearts that are acceptable unto You. In the Name of Jesus we pray. Amen.

## HOW TO SAY IT

Privy          **PRI**-vee.

Cyprus          **SAI**-pris.

## PREPARE FOR NEXT SUNDAY

Read **Acts 5:27–29, 33–42** and "Witnessing to the Truth."

---

**DAILY HOME BIBLE READINGS**

**MONDAY**
Rescuing the Weak
(Psalm 82)

**TUESDAY**
Living Blamelessly
(Psalm 26)

**WEDNESDAY**
Sharing Generously
(1 Timothy 5:11–19)

**THURSDAY**
Sharing with All
(Isaiah 1:15–18)

**FRIDAY**
Sharing Troubles
(Philippians 4:1–14)

**SATURDAY**
Sharing Out of Abundance
(Luke 3:10–16)

**SUNDAY**
Sharing All Things
(Acts 4:34–5:10)

**Sources:**

Carson, D.A., France, R.T., Motyer, J.A., Wenham, J.G. *New Bible Commentary*. Downers Grove, IL: InterVarsity Press, 1993.

Keener, Craig S. *IVP Bible Background Commentary*. Downers Grove, IL: InterVarsity Press, 1993.

Polhill, John B. Acts. *New American Commentary: An Exegetical and Theological Exposition of Holy Scripture*. Nashville: B&H Publishing, 1992.

## COMMENTS / NOTES:

_____

_____

_____

_____

_____

_____

_____

_____

_____

_____

_____

_____

_____

_____

_____

_____

_____

_____

_____

_____

# WITNESSING TO THE TRUTH

**BIBLE BASIS:** ACTS 5:27–29, 33–42

**BIBLE TRUTH:** The apostles knew that they were obeying God's calling, even when the authorities tried to stop them.

**MEMORY VERSE:** "Then Peter and the other apostles answered and said, We ought to obey God rather than men" (Acts 5:29).

**LESSON AIM:** By the end of this lesson we will: EXAMINE the apostles' proclamation of Jesus as the Messiah despite being ordered not to do so by the Sanhedrin; ASSESS our commitment to witnessing and proclaiming the name of Jesus; and IDENTIFY and overcome barriers to evangelism efforts within and without the church community.

## LESSON SCRIPTURE

### ACTS 5:27–29, 33–42, KJV

27 And when they had brought them, they set them before the council: and the high priest asked them,

28 Saying, Did not we straitly command you that ye should not teach in this name? and, behold, ye have filled Jerusalem with your doctrine, and intend to bring this man's blood upon us.

29 Then Peter and the other apostles answered and said, We ought to obey God rather than men.

33 When they heard that, they were cut to the heart, and took counsel to slay them.

34 Then stood there up one in the council, a Pharisee, named Gamaliel, a doctor of the law, had in reputation among all the people, and commanded to put the apostles forth a little space;

35 And said unto them, Ye men of Israel, take heed to yourselves what ye intend to do as touching these men.

36 For before these days rose up Theudas, boasting himself to be somebody; to whom a number of men, about four hundred, joined themselves: who was slain; and all, as many as obeyed him, were scattered, and brought to nought.

37 After this man rose up Judas of Galilee in the days of the taxing, and drew away much people after him: he also perished; and all, even as many as obeyed him, were dispersed.

38 And now I say unto you, Refrain from these men, and let them alone: for if this counsel or this work be of men, it will come to nought:

39 But if it be of God, ye cannot overthrow it; lest haply ye be found even to fight against God.

40 And to him they agreed: and when they had called the apostles, and beaten them, they commanded that they should not speak in the name of Jesus, and let them go.

41 And they departed from the presence of the council, rejoicing that they were counted worthy to suffer shame for his name.

42 And daily in the temple, and in every house, they ceased not to teach and preach Jesus Christ.

## LIFE NEED FOR TODAY'S LESSON

**AIM: You will learn that some people are so dedicated to a cause that they will go to any lengths, even enduring pain and suffering, to achieve their goals.**

## INTRODUCTION

### Teaching in Difficult Times

The fifth chapter of Acts gives an account of the powerful ministry of the apostles. The apostles had been commissioned by Jesus Himself to teach and be witnesses in **Matthew 28:19–20**. Following the outpouring of the Holy Spirit, the apostles taught powerfully, and their teaching was accompanied by signs and wonders. The high priest and the Sadducees were filled with jealousy and had Peter and John arrested. However, an angel appeared to them during the night, freed them, and instructed them to teach the Word of Life, the words of salvation and eternal life. At this time, Christianity was called "The Way" and "The Life" (**Acts 9:2**).

## BIBLE LEARNING

**AIM: You will learn that believers can develop a stronger commitment to God and a willingness to follow Christ.**

## I. CHOOSING TO OBEY GOD (Acts 5:27–29)

The Sanhedrin forbid Peter and John from teaching in the name of Jesus (**Acts 4:18**). However, Jesus had given them a mandate to teach. An angel had further instructed them the previous night. Knowing that it could result in persecution, the apostles continue to "fill Jerusalem" with their teaching and perform signs and wonders. The apostles have already been imprisoned and seen the treatment Jesus received for going against the religious establishment. The apostles are very aware of the danger of spreading their message. Staring into the face of persecution and possibly death, the apostles consciously choose to obey God, even at personal cost to themselves.

### Acts 5:27–29, 33–42

27 And when they had brought them, they set them before the council: and the high priest asked them, 28 Saying, Did not we straitly command you that ye should not teach in this name? and, behold, ye have filled Jerusalem with your doctrine, and intend to bring this man's blood upon us. 29 Then Peter and the other apostles answered and said, We ought to obey God rather than men.

The disciples had been arrested and imprisoned the night before. They were now apprehended again in the morning. Having placed the disciples before the Sanhedrin, the high priest brings a threefold charge against them.

First, the apostles are accused of violating the previous injunction given to them not to preach in the name of Jesus. The phrase translated here as "straitly command" in Greek is *paraggelia paraggello* (**pah-ron-ghe-LEE-ah pah-ron-GHEL-loh**) or "to command a command." Use of a verb with its cognate dative like this can emphasize the idea of the verb. So rather than just being "commanded," they were "straitly commanded." The apostles were violating the authority of the high priest, who was the de facto ruler over the Jewish nation.

Second, it is a grievous accusation that the apostles had "filled" (Gk. *pleroo*, **play-ROW-oh**) Jerusalem with their doctrine. This word means to fill up to the full or completely. The apostles had filled Jerusalem with the teaching of Christ's death and resurrection. In just a short time, all Jerusalem knew of Christ's resurrection.

Lastly, the Sanhedrin claims the apostles mean to blame the council for Jesus' death. The Sanhedrin might say this intending to insinuate the disciples were inciting the populace to sedition, but more clearly they are revealing their own guilty consciences.

## SEARCH THE SCRIPTURES

### QUESTION 1

What is the name of the council that Peter and the other apostles had to appear before? How many charges were brought against them?

## II. WORDS OF CAUTION (vv. 33–39)

The Sanhedrin is in a difficult situation. On one hand, they are furious with the apostles for teaching and healing in Jesus' name and even more so for defying their orders. On the other hand, they fear the people and do not want to upset them. The Sanhedrin wants to kill the apostles, but Gamaliel, the most prominent rabbi of their time, cautions them not to act on their wishes (vv. 34–36).

Gamaliel urges the council to proceed with caution. Theudas and Judas had come and caused the people to revolt, but when they were killed, their followers scattered. Unfortunately, Gamaliel put Jesus in the same category as the impostors. He felt that, given enough time, Jesus' followers would also disband. Gamaliel also acknowledges the possibility that the apostles were sent from God. He understands that if, indeed, the apostles are from God, the Sanhedrin will not be able to stop them.

33 When they heard that, they were cut to the heart, and took counsel to slay them. 34 Then stood there up one in the council, a Pharisee, named Gamaliel, a doctor of the law, had in reputation among all the people, and commanded to put the apostles forth a little space; 35 And said unto them, Ye men of Israel, take heed to yourselves what ye intend to do as touching these men. 36 For before these days rose up Theudas, boasting himself to be somebody; to whom a number of men, about four hundred, joined themselves: who was slain; and all, as many as obeyed him, were scattered, and brought to nought. 37 After this man rose up Judas of Galilee in the days of the taxing, and drew away much people after him: he also perished; and all, even as many as obeyed him, were dispersed. 38 And now I say unto you, Refrain from these men, and let them alone: for if this counsel or this work be of men, it will come to nought: 39 But if it be of God, ye cannot overthrow it; lest haply ye be found even to fight against God.

When the members of the Sanhedrin hear Peter's response (vv. 29–32), they are cut to the heart or "enraged" (RSV). The Greek verb diaprio (dee-ah-PREE-oh) translated here as "cut to the heart" has the root meaning of being "sawn through." It is found only here and in verse 7:54. It means that they were violently enraged, indicating a state of very sharp vexation resulting in inward rage. It is a situation where personal rage dethrones reason. Like wounded and cornered beasts, the only recourse is to destroy their pursuers. So they resolve to kill the disciples.

When the Sanhedrin seemed likely to resort to violent measures against the apostles, Gamaliel, a Pharisee among them, intervenes. He was a kindly man who was loved and respected, and, obviously, was more tolerant than his fellows. Had the Sanhedrin not been restrained by Gamaliel's cool and wise advice, they probably would have ordered the stoning of the disciples as they later did Stephen. Three important things are to be noted of Gamaliel: he was a Pharisee, a doctor of the law, and had a reputation among all the people. Hence he was best qualified and suited to defend the apostles. He was the teacher of Saul, who became Paul the apostle (**Acts 22:3**), and he was the grandson of Hillel, and the most influential rabbi of his time. Ancient Jewish scholars wrote of him that, "Since Rabban Gamaliel the elder died there has been no more reverence for the law; and purity and abstinence died out at the same time." Like his grandfather Hillel, he was noted for his liberal attitude.

## SEARCH THE SCRIPTURES
### QUESTION 2
Describe who was Gamaliel and his relationship to Peter and John.

## III. PERSECUTION AND JOY (vv. 40–42)

Bearing Gamaliel's warning in mind, the Sanhedrin calls the apostles in once again. They repeat their orders not to teach in the name of Jesus. Because they disobeyed the Sanhedrin's initial orders, the apostles are punished according to Jewish law, which called for thirty-nine lashes on bare skin with a leather whip. The beating not only gave vent to the Sanhedrin's fury but was intended to deter and shame the apostles. By bringing shame on the apostles, they hoped to also bring shame on those listening to their teaching.

Rather than being frightened or embittered, the apostles go away rejoicing. They are honored to suffer disgrace for the name of Jesus. Christ had warned them that persecution would come: "God blesses you when people mock you and persecute you and lie about you and say all sorts of evil things against you because you are my followers. Be happy about it! Be very glad! For a great reward awaits you in heaven. And remember, the ancient

prophets were persecuted in the same way" (**Matthew 5:11–12, NLT**). Not only do the apostles rejoice, they redouble their efforts. Every day they teach about Jesus (**v. 42**), whether in the Temple or in people's homes. The apostles joyfully follow Jesus' instructions knowing that they put themselves in danger by doing so.

**40 And to him they agreed: and when they had called the apostles, and beaten them, they commanded that they should not speak in the name of Jesus, and let them go. 41 And they departed from the presence of the council, rejoicing that they were counted worthy to suffer shame for his name. 42 And daily in the temple, and in every house, they ceased not to teach and preach Jesus Christ.**

The Sanhedrin listens to Gamaliel and once again, after threatening the apostles, lets them go, but this time with a flogging. The exact word for "beaten" (Gk. *dero*, **DEH-ro**) was originally used for flaying and skinning. It is also a general word for violent whipping. In other words, the apostles received a beating that left wounds on the skin. Flogging was the customary punishment used as a warning not to persist in an offense. It consisted of thirty-nine lashes, often referred to as the forty less one (cf. **2 Corinthians 11:24**), based on **Deuteronomy 25:3**. It was still a cruel punishment. With bared chest and in a kneeling position, one was beaten with a tripled strap of calf hide across both chest and back, two on the back for each stripe across the chest. Men were known to have died from the ordeal. As before, the apostles are warned not to continue their witness in Jesus' name. This time the warning is reinforced with somewhat stronger persuasion.

The apostles remain undeterred. They are determined to face whatever dangers threaten. They are not cowed by the council's threats and commands. The apostles continue to obey God rather than men. In fact, they rejoice at having suffered for Jesus' name. This word "suffer shame" (Gk. *atimazo*, **ah-ti-MAHD-zo**) means to suffer dishonor and disgrace. This psychological suffering serves as a counterpoint to the physical beating they received. And the witness to the name continues—publicly in the temple and privately in Christians' homes. They rejoice in persecution for two reasons. First, it is an opportunity to demonstrate their loyalty to Christ. Second, it is a real opportunity to share in the experience of Christ. Those who share in the cross-bearing will share in the crown-wearing.

## SEARCH THE SCRIPTURES

### QUESTION 3
Why did the apostles rejoice?

**The apostles rejoiced because they were counted worthy to suffer for the Gospel.**

## BIBLE APPLICATION

**AIM: You will understand the importance of developing a stronger commitment to God and a willingness to follow Christ.**

Many Christians in the United States are not willing to sacrifice their comfort, let alone their lives, for God. Around the world, Christians are persecuted, tortured, and killed for preaching Jesus. Christians are persecuted in over fifty countries, including imprisonment, torture, and martyrdom. The five counties that have the most severe persecution are North Korea, Somalia, Syria, Iraq, and Afghanistan. Still, the church is growing in these hostile nations. They follow the example of the apostles, most of whom paid for their obedience with their lives. The apostles were willing to do whatever it took to obey God. Are you?

## STUDENT'S RESPONSES

**AIM: You will learn that in spite of difficult times, you can depend on the Lord.**

Like the apostles, we are to continue to proclaim the name of Jesus even in difficult circumstances. They never stopped proclaiming the Good News of Christ even in the face of imprisonment and beatings. Even amid persecution, the apostles rejoiced because they valued their obedience to Jesus more than their safety or lives. They were determined to make Christ known even at great personal cost, and felt privileged to suffer for the name of Christ.

While we have relative freedom to share the Gospel in the United States, many do not have the same opportunity. Research different organizations that aid those in other countries who are persecuted, such as Voice of the Martyrs (http://www.persecution.com) or Open Doors USA (http://www.opendoorsusa.org). Look for opportunities to write to those who are suffering persecution for their faith in other countries.

## PRAYER

Dear Jesus, bless us to stand up with courage and conviction for knowing and believing in You and Your Word. Our determination to witness to others about who You are is a reflection of Your strength and life. In the Name of Jesus, we pray. Amen.

## HOW TO SAY IT

| | |
|---|---|
| Gamaliel. | gah-**mah-LEE**-ale. |
| Quirinius. | kwih-**RIN**-ee-uhs. |
| Rabban. | **RAH**-ban. |
| Theudas. | **THOO**-duhs. |

## PREPARE FOR NEXT SUNDAY

Read **Acts 7:2–4, 8–10, 17, 33–34, 45–47, 53** and "Remembering God's Faithfulness."

### DAILY HOME BIBLE READINGS

**MONDAY**
The Cause of Truth
(Psalm 45:1–4, 6–7)

**TUESDAY**
The Life of Truth
(Proverbs 14:22–29)

**WEDNESDAY**
The Power of Truth
(Luke 4:14–19)

**THURSDAY**
Avoid Foolishness; Live Truthfully
(2 Timothy 2:14–16, 22–26)

**FRIDAY**
Trustworthy and Truth
(Revelation 22:1–7)

**SATURDAY**
Prevailing Truth
(Acts 4:5–12)

**SUNDAY**
Witnessing the Truth
(Acts 5:27–29, 33–42)

**Sources:**

Alexander, Joseph A. *Commentary on Acts of the Apostles*. Grand Rapids: Zondervan Publishing House, 1956 (reprint).

Bruce, F. F. *The Book of the Acts*. The New International Commentary on the New Testament. Grand Rapids, Mich.: William B. Eerdmans Publishing Co., 1988.

Carter, Charles W. and Ralph Earle. *The Acts of the Apostles*. Salem, Ohio: Schmul Publishing Co., 1959.

Dockery, David S., ed. *Holman Concise Bible Commentary*. Nashville, TN: Broadman & Holman Publishers, 1998.

Henry, Matthew. *Matthew Henry's Commentary on the Whole Bible: Complete and Unabridged in One Volume*. Peabody: Hendrickson, 1994.

Johnson, Luke Timothy. *The Acts of the Apostles*. Sacra Pagina Series. Vol. 5, Collegeville, Minn.: Liturgical Press, 1992.

Marshall, I Howard. *The Acts of the Apostles: An Introduction and Commentary*. The Tyndale New Testament Commentaries. Grand Rapids, Mich.: W.B. Eerdmans Pub. Co., 1980.

Polhill, John B. *Acts*, vol. 26, *The New American Commentary*. Nashville: Broadman & Holman Publishers, 1995.

Schuerer, Emil. *A History of The Jewish People in the Time of Jesus Christ*. Edinburgh: T & T Clark, 1885.

Spence-Jones, H. D. M., ed. *Acts of the Apostles, The Pulpit Commentary, Vol. 1*. London; New York: Funk & Wagnalls Company, 1909.

*The Holy Bible: English Standard Version*. Wheaton: Standard Bible Society, 2001.

Utley, Robert James. *Luke the Historian: The Book of Acts. Vol. 3B*. Study Guide Commentary Series. Marshall, TX: Bible Lessons International, 2003.

Wiersbe, Warren W. *The Bible Exposition Commentary*. Wheaton, IL: Victor Books, 1996.

## COMMENTS / NOTES:

_____

_____

_____

_____

_____

_____

_____

_____

_____

_____

_____

_____

_____

_____

_____

_____

_____

_____

_____

_____

_____

_____

_____

_____

_____

_____

_____

_____

_____

_____

_____

_____

# REMEMBERING GOD'S FAITHFULNESS

**BIBLE BASIS:** ACTS 7:2–4, 8–10, 17, 33–34, 45–47, 53

**BIBLE TRUTH:** Stephen spoke to the council on the history of God's faithfulness.

**MEMORY VERSE:** "But he, being full of the Holy Ghost, looked up stedfastly into heaven, and saw the glory of God, and Jesus standing on the right hand of God" (Acts 7:55).

**LESSON AIM:** By the end of this lesson we will: STUDY Stephen's proclamation before the council in which he reminded the Jews of God's faithfulness through the ages and their disregard of God's Law; REFLECT on the meaning of beliefs and a willingness to stand firm in life-threatening circumstances; and COMMIT to stand for beliefs about God in all circumstances.

## LESSON SCRIPTURE

### ACTS 7:2–4, 8–10, 17, 33–34, 45–47, 53, KJV

2 And he said, Men, brethren, and fathers, hearken; The God of glory appeared unto our father Abraham, when he was in Mesopotamia, before he dwelt in Charran,

3 And said unto him, Get thee out of thy country, and from thy kindred, and come into the land which I shall shew thee.

4 Then came he out of the land of the Chaldaeans, and dwelt in Charran: and from thence, when his father was dead, he removed him into this land, wherein ye now dwell.

8 And he gave him the covenant of circumcision: and so Abraham begat Isaac, and circumcised him the eighth day; and Isaac begat Jacob; and Jacob begat the twelve patriarchs.

9 And the patriarchs, moved with envy, sold Joseph into Egypt: but God was with him,

10 And delivered him out of all his afflictions, and gave him favour and wisdom in the sight of Pharaoh king of Egypt; and he made him governor over Egypt and all his house.

17 But when the time of the promise drew nigh, which God had sworn to Abraham, the people grew and multiplied in Egypt,

33 Then said the Lord to him [Moses], Put off thy shoes from thy feet: for the place where thou standest is holy ground.

34 I have seen, I have seen the affliction of my people which is in Egypt, and I have heard their groaning, and am come down to deliver them. And now come, I will send thee into Egypt.

45 Which also our fathers that came after brought in with Jesus into the possession of the Gentiles, whom God drave out before the face of our fathers, unto the days of David;

46 Who found favour before God, and desired to find a tabernacle for the God of Jacob.

47 But Solomon built him an house.

53 Who have received the law by the disposition of angels, and have not kept it.

## LIFE NEED FOR TODAY'S LESSON

**AIM: You will learn that people will defend against all criticism of their beliefs, even if their life is in danger.**

## INTRODUCTION

### Stephen's Irritating Speech

Following the release of the apostles in Acts 5, the message of Christ continued to spread with power. The apostles chose seven men to serve, including Stephen, who were filled with the Spirit and wisdom. Today's lesson highlights some of Stephen's speech to the Sanhedrin after his arrest. He was charged with speaking blasphemy against God, His temple, and Moses. Stephen's response does not directly answer the Sanhedrin's charges; rather, he turns their charges against them and explains how they have rejected God. In addition to being full of the Spirit, Stephen was well acquainted with the Scriptures and the history of Israel. This made a powerful combination as he spoke before the Sanhedrin.

## BIBLE LEARNING

**AIM: You will learn how Stephen spoke critically and directly to his accusers, the Sanhedrin council.**

## I. THE LORD'S PROMISES TO ABRAHAM (Acts 7:2–4, 8)

While Stephen is accused of being a blasphemer and an apostate from the Jewish faith, he refers to Abraham as "our father Abraham," counting himself among the faithful. Stephen begins his discourse with the call of Abraham, the father of the Jewish faith. God calls Abraham out of Mesopotamia, which was filled with idol worship. Abraham's initial move was to Haran, where he remained until his father died five

years later. From there, he moved to Canaan. He was promised a son and given a covenant which was sealed with circumcision. When Isaac was born, he was circumcised on the eighth day. Isaac became the father of Jacob, who was the father of the patriarchs of the twelve tribes of Israel. God was faithful to the promise he made to Abraham that he would have a multitude of descendants.

## Acts 7:2–4, 8–10, 17, 33–34, 45–47, 53

**2 And he said, Men, brethren, and fathers, hearken; The God of glory appeared unto our father Abraham, when he was in Mesopotamia, before he dwelt in Charran, 3 And said unto him, Get thee out of thy country, and from thy kindred, and come into the land which I shall shew thee. 4 Then came he out of the land of the Chaldaeans, and dwelt in Charran: and from thence, when his father was dead, he removed him into this land, wherein ye now dwell.**

Stephen has been falsely accused of blasphemy (**6:13**). The high priest, acting as the leader of the Sanhedrin, demanded to know whether the accusations were true or not (**7:1**). What follows in the rest of **Chapter 7** is Stephen's response. Although Stephen's speech in **Acts 7** has often been referred to as his speech before the Sanhedrin, it is more than that—it is his restatement of the teachings that have caused much irritation and resentment. It is notable that although Stephen would disagree with his audience, he began his speech with great deference to his hearers. He started by reminding them that they were his Jewish "brothers" and showed respect to the members of the Sanhedrin by referring to them as "fathers." The elders of Israel were thought of as fathers who ruled the nation. The opening words, "the God of glory" (Gk. *theos tes doxes*, **the-AHS tays DOK-says**), or the God who revealed Himself, are an implied answer to the accusation of blaspheming God. It is no accident that Stephen describes God as such, for His glory is seen in His self-manifestation, which was usually connected to the temple. Alexander gives an excellent explanation of the phrase as: "The God of glory, not merely the glorious [wonderful] God, or the God worthy to be glorified (**Psalm 29:1; Revelation 4:11**), but more specifically, that God who sensibly revealed himself of old, which is a standing sense of glory... in the Old Testament." It is the God of Glory who appeared (Gk. *optanomai*, **op-TAH-no-my**) or caused Himself to be seen. Thus Stephen identifies himself with the religious faith of his audience.

He then quickly moves into his survey of patriarchal history by quoting **Genesis 12:1**, God's call to Abraham to leave land and relatives and travel to a land to which He would direct him. God revealed Himself to Abraham in His full glory, even in a pagan land. Although **Genesis 12:1** is set in the context of Abraham's residency in Haran, Stephen placed the call in an earlier context when Abraham lived in Ur before ever leaving for Haran (**Genesis 11:31**), a conclusion one could draw from **Genesis 15:7**. By thus stressing that the call came to Abraham at the very beginning, Stephen implicitly made the point that God was in control of Abraham's entire movement. Stephen must have understood that the words of God to Terah in **Genesis 11:31** were similar to those in **Genesis 12:1**. In obedience to God, Abraham with his father Terah left the land of Chaldea (the same as Mesopotamia) and resided in Haran. Abraham promptly and cheerfully obeyed God. He did not know where he was going (**Hebrews 11:8**), but at the call of God he set forth promptly and willingly. We ought to learn a lesson from Abraham. When God distinctly speaks to us, whatever He may bid us do, at whatever cost we may be required to obey, it is only fitting for us to comply instantly and cheerfully. From Haran, God called Abraham into "this land where you are now living" (**v. 4**).

**8 And he gave him the covenant of circumcision: and so Abraham begat Isaac, and circumcised him the eighth day; and Isaac begat Jacob; and Jacob begat the twelve patriarchs.**

**Verse 8** is a transition verse, showing the beginnings of the fulfillment of God's promises to Abraham and leading into the history of the patriarchs. The covenant of circumcision (**Genesis 17:10–14**) implies the begetting (Gk. *gennao*, **geh-NAH-oh**) or fathering of children, and the circumcision of Isaac confirms that God kept His promise to give descendants to Abraham (**Genesis 21:4**). Stephen moved quickly through the patriarchal history using the motif of circumcision, from Isaac to Jacob to the twelve patriarchs. The stage was now set for the next step in Stephen's promise-fulfillment pattern: the story of Joseph.

## II. THE LORD'S DELIVERANCE THROUGH JOSEPH (vv. 9–10)

As he continues the history of God's work in Israel, Stephen then describes the story of Joseph. Joseph's brothers sold him into slavery in Egypt. However, God accomplishes His purposes in spite of them.

God was with Joseph and delivered him from his troubles. He found favor in the Pharaoh's sight and was placed in a position of authority. In turn, God used Joseph's position to deliver the patriarchs in a time of famine. The patriarchs sojourned in Egypt, which was a fulfillment of God's proclamation that they would be sojourners in a land that was not their own (**vv. 6–7**). God was faithful to every word He had spoken.

9 And the patriarchs, moved with envy, sold Joseph into Egypt: but God was with him, 10 And delivered him out of all his afflictions, and gave him favour and wisdom in the sight of Pharaoh king of Egypt; and he made him governor over Egypt and all his house.

Stephen recounts the story of Joseph— Joseph's being sold into Egypt out of envy (Gk. *zeloo*, **zay-LOH-oh**) or boiling hatred and anger by his brothers, his deliverance from affliction and rise to power in Egypt, the two visits of his brothers in the time of famine, and finally the descent of Jacob's whole clan into Egypt (**vv. 9–15**). Although Joseph suffered much in Egypt, God was with him (**v. 9**) even in his afflictions (Gk. *thlipsis*, **THLEEP-sees**). The word for "afflictions" means pressure or being pressed together, and metaphorically oppression, distress, and anything which causes one to feel pressured. Stephen's story of Joseph shows that God could not be limited to the temple. He was rejected and cast aside by his brothers, but God revealed himself to Joseph, even in Egypt. Although the Genesis narrative has much to say about Joseph's suffering, Stephen chooses not to dwell on this, instead stressing God's presence with Joseph. God fulfilled His promises through Joseph, delivering Israel from famine by his hand and granting him "favour and wisdom." This word "favour" (Gk. *charis*, **KHA-rees**) is also translated "grace" in other places in the New Testament (**Luke 2:40; Ephesians 2:8**). It is God's unmerited favor, which was given to Joseph in the court of Pharaoh. Though Joseph was characterized by wisdom and favor, his brothers were marked by jealousy, which led them to sell Joseph into Egypt (**v. 9**). Significantly, Stephen did not identify them as Joseph's "brothers" but rather as "the patriarchs," the fathers of Israel.

## SEARCH THE SCRIPTURES

### QUESTION 1
Stephen calls Joseph's brothers by their names or patriarchs?

### QUESTION 2
Joseph was granted what by God?

## III. THE LORD'S DELIVERANCE THROUGH MOSES (vv. 17, 33–34, 45–47)

Stephen then touches on the story of Moses, who fulfilled God's promise to deliver Israel. The Exodus and the establishment of the tabernacle were major points in Jewish history. Stephen describes the way that Moses was commissioned and that his coming was the fulfillment of promise. Again, God intervened in Israel's history to show His kindness and faithfulness. The Israelites were delivered from bondage in Egypt, sustained in the wilderness, and given the Law; yet they rejected God by rejecting Moses (e.g., **Numbers 14:12, Exodus 16:3**).

After the Exodus, the Lord established the tabernacle with Israel. The Jews accused Stephen of speaking against the temple because they equated the temple with the presence of God. However, Stephen demonstrates that the presence of God was with His people long before the temple was built.

17 But when the time of the promise drew nigh, which God had sworn to Abraham, the people grew and multiplied in Egypt. 33 Then said the Lord to him, Put off thy shoes from thy feet: for the place where thou standest is holy ground. 34 I have seen, I have seen the affliction of my people which is in Egypt, and I have heard their groaning, and am come down to deliver them. And now come, I will send thee into Egypt.

God never fails to act on time. The descendants of Jacob continued to live in Egypt and multiply until the time was near for the fulfillment of God's promise to Abraham. It was not the divine plan that Israel remain in Egypt surrounded by paganism, so God permitted the Israelites to be enslaved and maltreated until they would be ready and glad to leave Egypt. Eighty years before their departure, their deliverer Moses was born. Preserved from death in infancy, God later prepared him for the momentous and monumental task with forty years of royal training in leadership in Pharaoh's palace. It was followed by forty years of learning patience and submission in the wilderness. As the time of promise was drawing near, God was at work. This was the promise of Abraham that Stephen already quoted.

Stephen recounts Moses' encounter with God in **Exodus 3:1–10**. God commanded Moses to remove his sandals because he was standing on holy ground (**v. 33, Exodus 3:5**). Stephen's inclusion of this detail may have been a subtle reminder to his hearers that there was holy ground elsewhere, far from the temple in Jerusalem. God's self-revelation was and is not confined to Jewish soil in particular or anywhere in general. In other words, no place on earth is innately holy. The message Moses received was that of God's faithfulness to His promise to the patriarchs and His awareness of the distress of their descendants in Egypt. God was about to deliver them through the hand of Moses.

**45 Which also our father that came after brought in with Jesus into the possession of the Gentiles, whom God drave out before the face of our fathers, unto the days of David; 46 Who found favour before God, and desired to find a tabernacle for the God of Jacob. 47 But Solomon built him an house.**

Stephen replies to the charges of blasphemy against the temple by showing that the Israelites worshiped God in the wilderness in the tabernacle, which was God's pattern for the temple (a later construction of Solomon's). God gave the guidelines and pattern to Moses. It remained the place of worship after the conquest under Jesus (Gk. *Iesous*, **ee-ye-SOOS**). This name means "God is salvation." While in the New Testament it is used most often for Christ, it is also a Greek transliteration of Joshua, the captain of the Israelites who brought the nation into the Promised Land. From his time onwards, the tabernacle remained in the land, passed down from generation to generation until the time of David. The word for tabernacle is *skenoma* (Gk. **SKAY-no-mah**), which is a pitched tent or booth. By highlighting its mobile nature, Stephen clearly implies that the true spiritual worship of God is not confined to allocation or material buildings, and that in the same way that God was worshiped in the wilderness before there was a temple, so He may be worshiped now without a temple.

## SEARCH THE SCRIPTURES

### QUESTION 3
Stephen was charged with _____.

## IV. ISRAEL'S REJECTION (v. 53)

In his discourse, Stephen shows the Sanhedrin that they have been resisting God from the beginning. The Jews were quick to identify themselves as children of Abraham, but they failed to demonstrate the faith of Abraham. They felt that their biological ties to Abraham took precedence over their personal faith in his God.

The Jewish council was guilty of the same sin their forefathers committed: rejecting those sent by God. Stephen turns the council's own charges against them. They were the sons of the murderers of the prophets and they were following in their father's footsteps by killing Jesus.

**53 Who have received the law by the disposition of angels, and have not kept it.**

The whole purpose of Stephen's speech now becomes clear. He ends with a declaration of Israel's rebellion. By rejecting Christ, the Jewish leaders had filled up the measure of their fathers. Stephen's historical narrative had illustrated Israel's constant rejection of God's chosen leaders that climaxed in their treatment of Jesus. In its earliest days as a nation, Israel disobeyed the law of God, although it had received the law by the disposition (Gk. *diatage*, **dee-ah-tah-GAY**) or ordinance of angels. This is nowhere mentioned in the biblical text but is found in rabbinical sources. Moses, Joseph, and the prophets are all types of and pointers to Christ in that they were sent by God and rejected by their own people. Stephen pointed out to his hearers that they had already rejected and killed Christ and they needed to repent.

## SEARCH THE SCRIPTURES

### QUESTION 4
Stephen accused the leaders of deliberately _____ God's Law "that was given through _____" (**NIV, v. 53**).

## BIBLE APPLICATION

**AIM: You will experience the faithfulness of God and share your experiences with others.**

The people of Israel had been rejecting God throughout the years despite His faithfulness to them. Rather than seeing the Law as a beginning, the Jews refused to accept anything new. They had become so entrenched in religious traditions that the Jews did not recognize the Truth when He came to them.

As Christians filled with the Holy Spirit, we recognize that God does not reside in buildings. His Spirit is boundless. We have received the truth of God's Word in Jesus Christ. Like Stephen, we are to proclaim the truth of Christ in all circumstances. Stephen became the Church's first martyr because he witnessed to the truth. Like Stephen, let us remember God's faithfulness to His people throughout history, embrace the truth of Christ, and proclaim the truth boldly.

## STUDENT'S RESPONSES

**AIM: You will discover that Christians should commit and live out your commitment for Christ at all times.**

Like Stephen, we should study the Scriptures and learn about the faithfulness of God. We should respect customs and traditions but not idolize them, nor should we become so fixated on them that we miss what God is doing today. Compare and contrast what it would mean to insist on traditions or being stubborn versus taking a legitimate stand for what is right because of a biblical principle.

## PRAYER

Dear God, we pray for those who stand up for their beliefs in You. Thank You for Your protection and care for believers who are able to share the "Good News" of Christ. In the Name of Jesus we pray. Amen.

## HOW TO SAY IT

| | |
|---|---|
| Chaldea. | kal-**DEE**-uh. |
| Charran. | **KAIR**-uhn. |
| Mesopotamia | me-soh-puh-**TAY**-mee-uh. |

Sanhedrin.     san-**HEE**-drihn.

Tabernacle.     **TAB**-uhr-na-kul.

## PREPARE FOR NEXT SUNDAY

Read **Acts 5:27–29, 33–42** and "Witnessing to the Truth."

---

### DAILY HOME BIBLE READINGS

#### MONDAY
Remembering God's Commands
(Deuteronomy 7:1–11)

#### TUESDAY
Remembering God's Love
(Psalm 31:1–5, 19–24)

#### WEDNESDAY
Remembering God's Word
(Psalm 119:89–94)

#### THURSDAY
Remembering God's Grace
(1 Corinthians 1:1–9)

#### FRIDAY
Remembering God's Will
(1 Thessalonians 5:16–25)

#### SATURDAY
Responding to God's Faithfulness
(Acts 6:7–15)

#### SUNDAY
Remembering God's Faithfulness
(Acts 7:2–4, 8–10, 17, 33–34, 45–47, 53)

**Sources:**

Alexander, Joseph A. *Commentary on Acts of the Apostles.* Grand Rapids, MI: Zondervan, 1956.

Arrington, French L. *The Acts of the Apostles: An Introduction and Commentary.* Peabody, MA: Hendrickson, 1988.

Bruce, F. F. *The Book of the Acts. The New International Commentary on the New Testament.* Grand Rapids, MI: William B. Eerdmans Publishing Co., 1988.

Henry, Matthew. *Matthew Henry's Commentary on the Whole Bible: Complete and Unabridged in One Volume.* Peabody, MA: Hendrickson, 1994.

Jamieson, Robert, A. R. Fausset, and David Brown. *Commentary Critical and Explanatory on the Whole Bible.* Oak Harbor, WA: Logos Research Systems, Inc., 1997.

Johnson, Luke Timothy. *The Acts of the Apostles.* Sacra Pagina Series. Vol. 5. Collegeville, MN: Liturgical Press, 1992.

Marshall, I Howard. *The Acts of the Apostles: An Introduction and Commentary.* The Tyndale New Testament Commentaries. Grand Rapids, MI: William B. Eerdmans Publishing Co., 1980.

Polhill, John B. *Acts.* The New American Commentary, vol. 26. Nashville, TN: Broadman & Holman Publishers, 1995.

Wiersbe, Warren W. *The Bible Exposition Commentary.* Wheaton, IL: Victor Books, 1996.

## COMMENTS / NOTES:

# THE SPIRIT IS NOT FOR SALE

**BIBLE BASIS:** Acts 8:9–24

**BIBLE TRUTH:** Peter claims that inspiring speakers have spiritual power when one's heart is right before God.

**MEMORY VERSE:** "Then answered Simon, and said, Pray ye to the LORD for me, that none of these things which ye have spoken come upon me" (Acts 8:24).

**LESSON AIM:** By the end of this lesson we will: RECALL the proclamation of the Good News of Jesus Christ to reveal the power of the Holy Spirit; AFFIRM the necessity of being right with God in order to receive spiritual power from God; and DECIDE and act on witnessing to others about the power of the Holy Spirit.

## LESSON SCRIPTURE

### ACTS 8:9–24, KJV

9 But there was a certain man, called Simon, which beforetime in the same city used sorcery, and bewitched the people of Samaria, giving out that himself was some great one:

10 To whom they all gave heed, from the least to the greatest, saying, This man is the great power of God.

11 And to him they had regard, because that of long time he had bewitched them with sorceries.

12 But when they believed Philip preaching the things concerning the kingdom of God, and the name of Jesus Christ, they were baptized, both men and women.

13 Then Simon himself believed also: and when he was baptized, he continued with Philip, and wondered, beholding the miracles and signs which were done.

14 Now when the apostles which were at Jerusalem heard that Samaria had received the word of God, they sent unto them Peter and John:

15 Who, when they were come down, prayed for them, that they might receive the Holy Ghost:

16 (For as yet he was fallen upon none of them: only they were baptized in the name of the Lord Jesus.)

17 Then laid they their hands on them, and they received the Holy Ghost.

18 And when Simon saw that through laying on of the apostles' hands the Holy Ghost was given, he offered them money,

19 Saying, Give me also this power, that on whomsoever I lay hands, he may receive the Holy Ghost.

20 But Peter said unto him, Thy money perish with thee, because thou hast thought that the gift of God may be purchased with money.

21 Thou hast neither part nor lot in this matter: for thy heart is not right in the sight of God.

22 Repent therefore of this thy wickedness, and pray God, if perhaps the thought of thine heart may be forgiven thee.

**23** For I perceive that thou art in the gall of bitterness, and in the bond of iniquity.

**24** Then answered Simon, and said, Pray ye to the LORD for me, that none of these things which ye have spoken come upon me.

## LIFE NEED FOR TODAY'S LESSON

**AIM: You will better understand why people gather to hear inspiring speakers.**

## INTRODUCTION

### Spreading the Good News

The book of Acts begins with the outpouring of the promised Holy Spirit and the commencement of the proclamation of the Gospel of Jesus Christ. The book of Acts provides an eye witness account of the birth and spread of the church. The Gospel first went to the Jews; but some of them, rejected it. A remnant of the Jews, of course, gladly received the Good News. Although the early disciples experienced resistance from Jews in many places, they also encountered many who believed the gospel and converted, and it is because of the work of primarily Jewish disciples that the gospel was spread to the Gentiles as well. God's plan was to spread the gospel from Jerusalem to Judea, Samaria, and the ends of the earth (**Acts 1:8**). One strong proponent for spreading the Good News was Philip, who became known as "the Evangelist." The designation is well deserved, for when the Jerusalem Christians were scattered by the persecution led by Saul of Tarsus, Philip went to the city of Samaria and proclaimed the gospel with such power that a great number of people joyfully turned to Christ (**Acts 8:1–8**).

## BIBLE LEARNING

**AIM: You will discover that Peter believes that inspiring speakers are those whose hearts are right before God.**

## I. CONNED BY THE POWER OF DECEPTION (vv. 9–13)

Many people in the first century were influenced by enchanters and magicians. The so-called miracle workers were empowered by the enemy, Satan, and performed acts of exorcisms and healings (**Matthew 24:24; 2 Thessalonians 2:9**). These sorcerers used trickery and magic to deceive their audiences. Most acts were preformed for financial gain. Unfortunately, much of this same kind of dishonesty operates in modern-day churches and pulls overwhelming audience participation. Some Christians are still looking for "quick fixes" and are naïve when it comes to the power of God. They cannot discern when someone is functioning from authentic spiritual power that originates only through Jesus Christ, and are blind by the power of deception and fall victims to financial fraud. The power that comes from Christ is genuine, loving, and sincere and should not be commercialized for profit.

**9 But there was a certain man, called Simon, which beforetime in the same city used sorcery, and bewitched the people of Samaria, giving out that himself was some great one: 10 To whom they all gave heed, from the least to the greatest, saying, This man is the great power of God. 11 And to him they had regard, because that of long time he had bewitched them with sorceries. 12 But when they believed Philip preaching the things concerning the kingdom of God, and the name of Jesus Christ, they were baptized, both men and women. 13 Then Simon himself believed also: and when he was baptized, he continued with Philip, and wondered, beholding the miracles and signs, which were done.**

For some time before Philip arrived in Samaria, the town had been "bewitched" (Gk. *existemi*, **ex-IS-tay-mee**) by a man named Simon. The word "existemi" means to throw out of place. In this context it meant that the people of Samaria were amazed, astonished, and thrown into wonderment. He practiced witchcraft or "sorcery" (Gk. *mageuo*, **mah-GEW-oh**). Simon used his magical skills to persuade the people of Samaria that he was somebody great (cf. **5:36**). According to church tradition, Simon was said to have traveled to Rome and begun a Gnostic sect called the Simonians. This group was said to have erected a statue in his honor and worshiped him as a god, as well as his consort Helena as a goddess. Although we cannot confirm whether Simonians are directly connected to Simon Magus, this tradition supports the claim of Acts that he made himself to be "some great one."

Luke adds that as a result of the Samaritans' bewitchment they all gave heed (*prosecho*, **pro-SEH-kho**). This word literally means to bring or be with. In this context it means to turn the mind or attention to. Through his signs and wonders, Simon gained a following all over Samaria. We do not know whether at this time Simon had a particular doctrine, but we can see he had a significant influence over the population. Everyone, "the least" (Gk. *mikros*, **mi-KROS**) and "the greatest" (Gk. *megas*, **MEH-gas**), crowded around him, saying that Simon was in some way the special channel of the power of God or the supreme emanation of God Himself. This type of thought was totally antithetical to the Christian message, that Christ was shown to the be the power of God through His resurrection. In this environment, Philip was sent to preach and show people the genuine power of God in the Gospel message of Jesus Christ. For a long time the people "had regard," the same word used in **verse 10** for

"they all gave heed." Here Luke underscores the influence Simon had by using the same word but attaching it to duration of time versus the wide range of people. They were devoted to Simon because he had used witchcraft to bewitch them.

Philip did not preach about himself. Philip was preaching (Gk. *euaggelizo*, **ew-ang-ghe-LEED-zo**) "the things concerning the kingdom of God, and the name of Jesus Christ." Here we see the early Christian message, about the kingdom of God and the name of Jesus Christ. In other words, the kingdom and the King. The Samaritans "believed" (Gk. *pisteuo*, **peest-EW-oh**) and "were baptized" (Gk. *baptizo*, **bap-TEED-zo**). In this way, they responded completely to the message of the Good News. They believed and showed it through baptsim.

It says that even Simon believed and was baptized. He followed Philip everywhere, amazed by the great signs and miracles he saw. After having amazed others with his magic practice he himself was amazed. In view of what is said later in **verse 21**, we do not know whether Simon really believed. The Bible language does not always make a distcintion between believing and professing to believe (cf. **James 2:19**). He may have been more amazed by Philip's healing power than by his message.

## SEARCH THE SCRIPTURES

### QUESTION 1
Describe Simon and what people said about his power.

## II. CONVERTED BY THE POWER OF THE HOLY SPIRIT (vv. 14–17)

Jewish believers still had doubt that Gentiles (non-Jews) and half-Jews were eligible candidates for the Holy Spirit. The apostles sent

Peter and John to investigate this new group of Samaritan believers. They had to keep this new group of believers from becoming disconnected from other disciples. It was necessary not only for the Samaritans' sake but also for the apostles to witness the amazing power of the Holy Spirit. Some biblical scholars believe this dramatic filling of the Spirit validated the importance of powerful and effective preaching of believers. The prevailing pride of some of the Jews was such that they despised the Samaritans and regarded the Gentiles as ceremonially unclean. Philip's preaching and the laying of hands by the Apostles reflected the way the Gospel penetrated social barriers and dissolved racial prejudices. This event also demonstrated that the grace of God in Christ Jesus is freely available to all.

**14 Now when the apostles which were at Jersualem heard that Samaria had received the word of God, they sent unto them Peter and John: 15 Who, when they were come down, prayed for them, that they might receive the Holy Ghost: 16 (For as yet he was fallen upon none of them: only they were baptized in the name of the Lord Jesus.) 17 Then laid they their hands on them, and they received the Holy Ghost.**

When the "apostles" (Gk. *apostolos*, ah-POS-toe-los) heard that Samaria had received (Gk. *dechomai*, **DEH-kho-my**) the Word of God, they "sent" (Gk. *apostello*, **ah-po-STEL-lo**; the Greek words for sent and apostle have the same root meaning, literally "the delegated, delegated") Peter and John, to investigate. . On one occasion, James and John had wanted to call fire down from heaven to consume a Samaritan city (cf. **Luke 9:51–56**). It was fitting that one of them should be a part of the delegation that now went to welcome the people of Samaria into the church.

When they arrived, they discovered that although the Samaritans had believed and had been baptized into the name of Jesus, they had not yet received the Holy Ghost. So they prayed for them that they might receive (Gk. *lambano*, **lam-BA-no**) the Holy Ghost. This verb for receive, "lambano" is used in two different ways. Usually in the narrative sense, it means to take or to grasp. The other sense is to passively receive and this is used quite often in the more theologically significant verses. Although this passage in Acts is a narrative, the second sense is in mind here as they are receiving something from God, not taking or grasping it. Here we see the Holy Spirit as something divinely given. This stands in contrast to Simon's later thinking that he could own the power of the Spirit and use this power for his own purposes.

The Holy Ghost had not yet come upon (Gk. *epipipto*, **eh-pee-PEEP-to**) any of the Samaritans. The word here means to literally "fall on with force." They had simply been baptized into the name of the Lord Jesus. This statement raises some questions that have caused much perplexity and division: How did the apostles know that the Samaritans had not received the Holy Ghost? In the light of **Acts 2:38**, how could the Samaritans have believed and been baptized and not received the Spirit? The Samaritan Christians' experience is the typical experience of Christian life. Becoming a Christian is a process consisting first of conversion and water baptism. Repentance is the initial part of the conversion. Notice how John the Baptist said that one must bring fruit mete for repentance in order to be a candidate for water baptism. The next part is sanctification, which prepares one to receive the gift, or baptism of the Holy Spirit.

In addition to praying for them, the apostles laid (Gk. *epitethemi*, **eh-pee-TEE-thay-mee**) their hands, thus identifying the people for whom they prayed with the rest of the church, particularly the mother church in Jerusalem.

In answer to their prayers, the believers received the Holy Ghost.

## III. CORRECTED BY THE POWER OF FORGIVENESS (vv. 18-24)

Our society values materialism. So it is no surprise that just about anything has a "price." The lesson of Simon the magician is instructive to those of any age who would presume to barter God's spiritual gifts in hope of personal gain. Simon practiced the art of deception because that is all he knew. His success in trickery prompted great courage. He thought money had the power to buy anything he wanted. When he offered Peter and John money in exchange for the gift of the Holy Spirit it provoked Peter's unequivocal rebuke. The Holy Spirit is not for sale. No amount of money can purchase salvation. To receive the gift of the Holy Spirit, one has to repent, turn from sin and ask God to come into his or her life. God's precious power is only achieved through repentance and belief in Jesus Christ. Simon's response to Peter's reprimand also shows his willingness to receive correction. He admitted his error and sought forgiveness. He recognized the authority given to Peter and John, and more importantly, he acknowledged the power behind the prayers of the righteous.

**18 Now when Simon saw that the Spirit was given through the laying on of the apostles' hands, he offered them money, 19 saying, "Give me this power also, so that anyone on whom I lay my hands may receive the Holy Spirit." 20 But Peter said to him, "May your silver perish with you, because you thought you could obtain the gift of God with money! 21 You have neither part nor lot in this matter, for your heart is not right before God. 22 Repent, therefore, of this wickedness of yours, and pray to the Lord that, if possible, the intent of your heart may be forgiven you.**

**23 For I see that you are in the gall of bitterness and in the bond of iniquity." 24 And Simon answered, "Pray for me to the Lord, that nothing of what you have said may come upon me."**

Simon mistook the power of the Holy Spirit as something that could be purchased with money. He misunderstood the Holy Spirit's purpose; it was not another magician's trick to manipulate and gather followers. Simon asked the apostles to give him the same "power" (*exousia*, **ek-zoo-SEE-ah**) or authority; in this context, the power of one who has sway over others. It is not clear whether Simon believed the power he would have would help him to control others or the Holy Spirit. Either way; he was mistaken, the Holy Spirit is God and cannot be controlled and manipulated out of personal self-interest.

Peter gives Simon a scathing rebuke not a curse, but more like a prediction. He explains that Simon could not buy the Spirit of God; it is a gift (*dorea*, **do-re-AH**). The word in the New Testament, always denotes a supernatural or spiritual gift from God. Simon thought it could be bought the same way you could buy anything else. Peter perceives Simon's spiritual dullness and lets him know he had no part (*meris*, **meh-REES**) or assigned share in the experience of the Holy Spirit. He also says Simon has no lot (*kleros*, **KLAY-ros**), which was the determining a person's share, as of an inheritance, through casting of lots. This was sometimes done by writing the names of individuals on broken pieces of wood or pottery, then placing them into a vase or garment and shaking them. The first one to fall out would be the person chosen for an assignment or to receive a share of wealth, land, etc. This was not done by chance. Peter uses both meris and kleros to make his point: Simon has no part by design or chance in the Holy Spirit through buying it.

Peter tells Simon to repent (Gk. *metanoeo*, **me-tuh-nah-EH-oh**), which is a command to change his mind. It is not enough to feel sorry for what he has done. He also has to come to a new understanding regarding supernatural powers and how the Holy Spirit is obtained. Peter uses two words related to intellect here. The first is *repent* and the second is *intent* (Gk. *epinoia*, **eh-pee-NOY-ah**), which is an idea or thought process. Simon must not only realize that what he has done is wrong and pray to God, he must also change his understanding and way of thinking so that such ideas no longer influence his mind or his actions. Peter's mention of the gall of bitterness may be a reference to **Deuteronomy 29:18**, which associates idolatry with bitterness and poison. Peter puts this gall in parallel with the bond of iniquity, suggesting that the two are one and the same. It is Simon's misunderstanding of the Holy Spirit that has ensnared him in a bitter pitfall of sin.

Simon's answer to Peter may have come from remorse and an attempt to avoid the condemnation Peter spoke about not a genuine desire to repent. He mentions nothing about his sin or believing in Christ; his main concern seems to be avoiding punishment. He also asks Peter to pray in his stead as opposed to trusting in Christ and seeking God in prayer himself.

## SEARCH THE SCRIPTURES

### QUESTION 2
How did Simon think he could "acquire" the Holy Spirit?

### QUESTION 3
Peter tells Simon that he has to _____ for asking to buy the Holy Spirit.

## BIBLE APPLICATION

**AIM: You will know that the main source of** power in being a witness for Christ is the Holy Spirit.

Religious charlatans have been around since ancient times. Many people fall prey to an assortment of scams. Christians are no exception. Some are victimized by charismatic individuals who pervert the gospel for profit. True Christian leadership draws others by the power of the Holy Spirit, not by false pretense. They are messengers of God who exalt the person of Jesus Christ.

## STUDENT'S RESPONSES

**AIM: You will see that Christians learn how to have the right attitude in regards to spiritual power from God.**

Often we are missing something in our spiritual life. It may be a sense of dryness or emptiness. This may be due to the absence of the Holy Spirit's ministry in our lives. Whether you are a new Christian or someone who is mature in the faith you are always in need of spiritual renewal. Pray for the Holy Spirit to fill and empower you to minister to others. Next share your experience with someone else and pray that they would receive the ministry of the Holy Spirit.

## PRAYER

Sweet Holy Spirit! Sweet Holy Spirit! You presence in our lives is amazing. We rejoice that You guide us and protect us each and every day. Although the world rejects God's presence and grace, we stand with the right attitude to serve You and worship. In the Name of Jesus we pray. Amen.

## HOW TO SAY IT

| | |
|---|---|
| Diaconate. | DEE-ah-ko-nayt. |
| Samaria | suh-ME-ree-uh. |

## PREPARE FOR NEXT SUNDAY

Read **Acts 9:19b–31** and "Saul Earns Credibility."

### DAILY HOME BIBLE READINGS

**MONDAY**
Never Moved
(Psalm 15)

**TUESDAY**
Be Content
(Hebrews 13:5–10)

**WEDNESDAY**
Stand Firm
(Ephesians 6:14–18)

**THURSDAY**
Stand Boldly
(Acts 13:52—14:3)

**FRIDAY**
Stand Regardless
(Acts 8:1–8)

**SATURDAY**
Stand Ready
(Acts 8:26–40)

**SUNDAY**
The Spirit is Not For Sale
(Acts 8:9–24)

**Sources:**
Keener, Craig S. *IVP Bible Background Commentary.* Downers Grove, IL: InterVarsity Press, 1993.
Carson, D.A., France, R.T., Motyer, J.A., Wenham, J.G. *New Bible Commentary.* Downers Grove, IL: InterVarsity Press, 1993.
Polhill, John B. *Acts.* New American Commentary: An Exegetical and Theological Exposition of Holy Scripture. Nashville: B&H Publishing, 1992.

## COMMENTS / NOTES:

# SAUL EARNS CREDIBILITY

**BIBLE BASIS:** ACTS 9:19b–31

**BIBLE TRUTH:** Saul's bold and powerful preaching caused the numbers of the church to increase.

**MEMORY VERSE:** "And straightway he preached Christ in the synagogues, that he is the Son of God" (Acts 9:20).

**LESSON AIM:** By the end of this lesson we will:

RECALL Saul's acceptance as a Christian and the reward of his zeal in preaching about Jesus; EXAMINE the church's willingness to accept and meaningfully include in the Body of Christ those whose background is perceived as being suspect and encourage their bold witness about the change in their lives; and CELEBRATE those whose lives were transformed by Jesus Christ and then became bold witnesses for His cause.

## LESSON SCRIPTURE

### ACTS 9:19b–31, KJV

**19b** Then was Saul certain days with the disciples which were at Damascus.

**20** And straightway he preached Christ in the synagogues, that he is the Son of God.

**21** But all that heard him were amazed, and said; Is not this he that destroyed them which called on this name in Jerusalem, and came hither for that intent, that he might bring them bound unto the chief priests?

**22** But Saul increased the more in strength, and confounded the Jews which dwelt at Damascus, proving that this is very Christ.

**23** And after that many days were fulfilled, the Jews took counsel to kill him:

**24** But their laying await was known of Saul. And they watched the gates day and night to kill him.

**25** Then the disciples took him by night, and let him down by the wall in a basket.

**26** And when Saul was come to Jerusalem, he assayed to join himself to the disciples: but they were all afraid of him, and believed not that he was a disciple.

**27** But Barnabas took him, and brought him to the apostles, and declared unto them how he had seen the Lord in the way, and that he had spoken to him, and how he had preached boldly at Damascus in the name of Jesus.

**28** And he was with them coming in and going out at Jerusalem.

**29** And he spake boldly in the name of the Lord Jesus, and disputed against the Grecians: but they went about to slay him.

**30** Which when the brethren knew, they brought him down to Caesarea, and sent him forth to Tarsus.

**31** Then had the churches rest throughout all Judaea and Galilee and Samaria, and were edified; and walking in the fear of the Lord, and in the comfort of the Holy Ghost, were multiplied.

## LIFE NEED FOR TODAY'S LESSON

AIM: You will learn that people who are effective advocates boldly tell others about their deepest convictions.

## INTRODUCTION

### Paul Saw the Light

Before Saul's great conversion, he witnessed the stoning of the first Christian martyr, Stephen. Stephen's death commenced the events that would culminate in Saul's conversion and commission as the Apostle to the Gentiles. This transformation had lasting significance in Saul's life; meticulous accounts of it are given in the book of Acts (**9:1–19, 22:1–21, 26:1–23**) and referenced in his own writings (**1 Corinthians 15:9; Galatians 1:13–17**). But as an oppressor of the church, Saul breathed threats and murder against the disciples of the Lord. He tried to abolish the church, imprisoning both male and female Christians. While traveling toward Damascus, a light from heaven shone around Saul and his traveling companions and they fell to the ground (**Acts 9:1–19**). Temporarily blinded, Saul was led into Damascus. There, the disciple Ananias and the Christian community forgave Saul, baptized him, and helped him through the bewildering event of his conversion.

## BIBLE LEARNING

**AIM: You will discover how Saul earned credibility among many of the believers.**

## I. TESTIFYING POWER OF GOD'S LOVE (Acts 9:19b–25)

The sincerity of a speaker makes his or her testimony powerful, believable, and influential. A testimony has greater credibility when the listener can attest to the enormous change in the speaker's life, and this is evidenced in Saul's life. The voice of Saul echoed in the ears of those who were once viewed as prey to his persecution. Now, the man who despised Christians has become one! The man who persecuted the church is a member of it! The one who denied the existence of the truth is teaching others to accept the same. His experience with Jesus was authentic. It is difficult to convince others to believe in something

we do not believe ourselves. When we have an encounter with God, one that radically changes our lives, it is difficult to keep the Good News to ourselves. Paul spent time studying Jesus and wasted no time in sharing the Gospel with others. Too often we want to wait until we feel thoroughly grounded in our faith before we speak to anyone about Jesus' goodness. It is essential that we, the Lord's disciples, spread the Good News and become advocates for the Lord. God has done a marvelous thing in our lives; He saved and redeemed us! Salvation alone is justification enough to testify of the Lord's unmerited grace and mercy.

Saul was a brilliant scholar and could masterfully articulate a convincing argument. However, what convinced his listener was the evidence of God operating in his life. Our testimony should be backed up by a changed life.

## Acts 9:19b–31

**19b Then was Saul certain days with the disciples which were at Damascus. 20 And straightway he preached Christ in the synagogues, that he is the Son of God. 21 But all that heard him were amazed, and said; Is not this he that destroyed them which called on this name in Jerusalem, and came hither for that intent, that he might bring them bound unto the chief priests? 22 But Saul increased the more in strength, and confounded the Jews which dwelt at Damascus, proving that this is very Christ.**

This passage discusses the account of Saul's conversion experience and his stay in Damascus with the disciples for several days after his baptism. Although he had an extensive knowledge of the Old Testament, Saul was still a new convert and needed further instructions concerning the teachings about Christ prior to his stepping out to reach others for Christ. Evidently he was soon ready, because we find him straightway (Gk. *eutheos*, **ew-THEH-ose**) or "at once" preaching in the Jewish synagogues that Jesus is the Son of God. Many attempts have been made to explain Saul's conversion vision, often in the form of rationalistic explanations, such as a thunderstorm outside Damascus, an epileptic seizure, or psychogenic blindness as the result of repressed guilt. All such ideas are merely speculative. What the accounts in **Galatians 1:15–17, 1 Corinthians 15:8–9**, and **Acts 9** picture is a radical conversion experience. Saul the persecutor was stopped dead in his tracks on the Damascus road. The crucified and risen Jesus showed Himself to Saul, who was completely transformed from persecutor to witness. The one who would be the captor of Christians became a captive of Christ. For Saul and for Luke (the author of Acts), a totally different man emerged from that vision of the risen Lord, and that is conversion. There is only one word with which one can describe Paul's experience—a miracle, the result of direct divine action. When all is said and done, both Saul and the book of Acts give strikingly similar pictures of his conversion.

Immediately following his conversion, Saul not only identifies himself with the disciples who resided in Damascus but also starts proclaiming Christ as the living "Son of God," a phrase which occurs in Acts only here, but which nevertheless became a central concept for Saul and his apostolic ministry (cf. **Romans 1:1–4**). The extent of the astonishment or amazement of his Jewish listeners in the synagogue is seen in the Greek word *existemi* (Gk., **ek-SEES-tay-mee**), which includes the root meaning of standing out of oneself. As it was in the case of Ananias (**vv. 13–14**), they simply could not believe that the former persecutor who sought to destroy (Gk. *portheo*, **por-THEH-oh**, to ravage or sack) the church had made such a radical about-face. Luke described him as "proving" (Gk. *sumbibazo*, **soom-bee-BAD-zo**) that Jesus is the Christ. The word, used only in Acts and Saul's letters, means to join or put together, demonstrate, or deduce, and seems to picture his joining Old Testament prophecies

with their fulfillment in Christ, thus demonstrating that Jesus was the Christ, the Messiah promised by God to Israel. The result was that Saul's Jewish listeners were confounded and unable to respond to Paul's skillful interpretations of the Scriptures.

**23 And after that many days were fulfilled, the Jews took counsel to kill him: 24 But their laying await was known of Saul. And they watched the gates day and night to kill him. 25 Then the disciples took him by night, and let him down by the wall in a basket.**

According to Paul's account in **Galatians 1:18**, in the third year after his conversion he went to Jerusalem. The "many days" here corresponds to that account. The expression "after three years" is probably an inclusive reckoning (**Galatians 1:18**). In Jewish reckoning, any part of a year was considered a year. "Three years" would thus refer to two full years and any portion of the third, from its beginning to its end, or even one full year and any portion of two others. It was during this period that Paul visited Arabia before returning to Damascus. Unable to refute Saul, the exasperated Jews in Damascus finally took counsel, that is, conspired to kill him. The Greek word *anaireo* (**ah-neye-REH-oh**) translated here as "kill" used here literally means to take away or to do away with. When Saul and the disciples learned of the plot, plans were made for assuring his escape from the Jews. Since the Jewish plotters must have been carefully watching the city gates for Saul, the disciples chose another route for his escape. He was lowered in a basket through the window of a house built along the city wall. Paul also referred to this event in **2 Corinthians 11:32–33**.

## II. TRANSFORMING POWER OF GOD'S LOVE (VV. 26–31)

Saul had a horrible reputation with fellow Christians. Many did not trust him and doubted the legitimacy of his transformation. Despite the naysayers, Saul continued to preach the Word of God with power and conviction. Saul's advocate, Barnabas, came alongside him and vouched for his authenticity. He journeyed with Saul and introduced him to the Apostles and other believers, who welcomed him into the community. Like Barnabas, it is essential that we rally behind new Christians who have tarnished reputations. Encouragement is essential to the growth of new believers. Reassurance stifles the pessimistic darts thrown by other followers who doubt their conversion. No matter how one has lived in the past, we must be willing to accept and welcome all of God's children into the family of faith. God has already accepted us and others into the fold, so who are we to deny membership to anyone? Saul's transforming life is an excellent example of the tremendous, incomprehensible, and unfailing love God has for humanity. God can change anyone; His grace and love do not discriminate. The person our society thinks is less deserving of forgiveness and transformation is a prime candidate to become an instrument for the Lord's divine purpose. Saul's zealous and bold proclamation of the Good News of Jesus Christ drew many to God; lives and communities were empowered. The church flourished and grew stronger as many decided to give their lives to Christ and live in fear of the Lord.

26 And when Saul was come to Jerusalem, he assayed to join himself to the disciples: but they were all afraid of him, and believed not that he was a disciple. 27 But Barnabas took him, and brought him to the apostles, and declared unto them how he had seen the Lord in the way, and that he had spoken to him, and how he had preached boldly at Damascus in the name of Jesus. 28 And he was with them coming in and going out at Jerusalem. 29 And he spake boldly in the name of the Lord Jesus, and disputed against the Grecians: but they went about to slay him. 30 Which when the brethren knew, they brought him down to Caesarea, and sent him forth to Tarsus. 31 Then had the churches rest throughout all Judaea and Galilee and Samaria, and were edified; and walking in the fear of the Lord, and in the comfort of the Holy Ghost, were multiplied.

On arriving in Jerusalem, Saul attempted to join up with the Christian community there but was at first rejected. Like Ananias, they knew his reputation as a persecutor and were not convinced that so vehement an enemy could now be a Christian brother. In character with what we learn of him in Acts, Barnabas enters the picture as mediator and facilitates the acceptance of Paul by taking him to the apostles and testifying to his conversion. Barnabas' testimony would fully rehabilitate Saul in the minds of the apostles. Thus he secured Saul's acceptance in the apostolic circle. Saul was now "with them coming in and going out among them" in Jerusalem (**v. 28**). The expression is reminiscent of **Acts 1:21,** where it refers to the circle of apostles. That meaning may well be intended here. Saul was fully accepted into the apostolic circle. He too was a "witness" for Christ. As he had previously done in Damascus, Saul testified in the synagogues and was resisted. This time Saul debated with his fellow "Grecians," or Greek-speaking Jews. One is reminded of Stephen, and it may have been in the same synagogue that Saul gave his testimony for Christ (cf. **6:9–10**). Earlier they had succeeded in having Stephen killed; now they determined to do the same to Saul. Again the plot to kill Saul leaked, and the Christians hastened Saul off to the port of Caesarea and from there to his hometown of Tarsus.

**Verse 31** concludes the story of Saul's conversion and the end of the persecution that broke out after Stephen's death (**8:1**). The persecution was now ended with the conversion of its most ardent advocate into a witness for Christ. The church throughout all of Judea, Galilee, and Samaria was at peace. Although the Jerusalem church was now decentralized, it was still regarded as unified. The "peace" (NLT) of the church is described in terms of edification (the building up of the believers), walking in the fear of the Lord (reverence and worship), the "comfort" (KJV) or "encouragement" (NLT) of the Spirit, and multiplication and growth, terms reminiscent of the earlier summaries in Acts (cf. **2:43–47**). It is a familiar pattern. The Lord brings His people through a time of crisis. Through His deliverance, the church finds peace and continues to flourish (cf. **5:42**).

## SEARCH THE SCRIPTURES

### QUESTION 1
What happened when Paul attempted to connect with apostles and the Christan community?

### QUESTION 2
How does Barnabas help others accept and feel more comfortable with Paul?

## BIBLE APPLICATION

AIM: **You will learn that Christians are able to have a bold and strong impact on the lives of others.**

All kinds of people go to the hospital: the educated and illiterate, poor and privileged, thieves and stellar citizens gather in one facility seeking medical assistance. The church is similar to a hospital. Regardless of a person's lifestyle or background, anyone in need of God's attention is invited to join. All are welcomed to receive the gift of life through accepting Christ Jesus as Lord and Savior. Believers should welcome new brothers and sisters into the family of faith.

## STUDENT'S RESPONSES

AIM: **You will acknowledge that Christians should not judge others by their past and neglect to see the power of the Holy Spirit in the lives of others.**

As ambassadors of Christ Jesus, we should declare boldly the life-changing experience we have in Him. People around us should know we are Christians. Our lives should reflect what we preach and inspire others to seek Christ. One of the ways we grow in our passion for telling others about our experience with Christ is to review the story of how we came to know Him. As a class, write out your individual testimonies of how you came to become a follower of Christ. Share your stories with the other class members.

## PRAYER

Lord, we are ambassadors of Your Holy Word. Guide our tongues and allow us to hear and see what we need to do as we share Your Word. Bless us and keep us. In the Name of Jesus, we pray. Amen.

## HOW TO SAY IT

Ananias.          a-nuh-**NEE**-uhs.

Barnabas.        **BAHR**-nuh-buhs.

## PREPARE FOR NEXT SUNDAY

Read **Acts 10:24–38** and "Peter Takes a Risk."

### DAILY HOME BIBLE READINGS

**MONDAY**
God's Perfect Way
(Psalm 18:20–30)

**TUESDAY**
God's Trustworthy Way
(Psalm 112:1–2, 6–9)

**WEDNESDAY**
God's Holy Way
(1 Peter 1:16–19)

**THURSDAY**
God's Generous Way
(Luke 11:32–36)

**FRIDAY**
God's Surprising Way
(Acts 9:1–9)

**SATURDAY**
God's Unconventional Way
(Acts 9:10–19)

**SUNDAY**
Saul Earns Credibility
(Acts 9:20–31)

**Sources:**
Carson, D.A., France, R.T., Motyer, J.A., Wenham, J.G. *New Bible Commentary.* Downers Grove, IL: InterVarsity Press, 1993.
Keener, Craig S. *IVP Bible Background Commentary.* Downers Grove, IL: InterVarsity Press, 1993.
Polhill, John B. Acts. *New American Commentary: An Exegetical and Theological Exposition of Holy Scripture.* Nashville: B&H Publishing, 1992.

## COMMENTS / NOTES:

# PETER TAKES A RISK

**BIBLE BASIS:** ACTS 10:24–38

**BIBLE TRUTH:** Peter's recognition that God shows no partiality allowed him to tell the Good News to the Gentiles.

**MEMORY VERSES:** "Then Peter opened his mouth, and said, Of a truth I perceive that God is no respecter of persons: But in every nation he that feareth him, and worketh righteousness, is accepted with him" (Acts 10:34–35).

**LESSON AIM:** By the end of the lesson, we will: BECOME aware that Peter told the Gentiles about the message of God's love; CELEBRATE that God loves all people; and FIND ways to communicate God's love to those who do not know Jesus Christ as Savior.

## LESSON SCRIPTURE

### ACTS 10:24–38, KJV

24 And the morrow after they entered into Cæsarea. And Cornelius waited for them, and had called together his kinsmen and near friends.

25 And as Peter was coming in, Cornelius met him, and fell down at his feet, and worshipped him.

26 But Peter took him up, saying, Stand up; I myself also am a man.

27 And as he talked with him, he went in, and found many that were come together.

28 And he said unto them, Ye know how that it is an unlawful thing for a man that is a Jew to keep company, or come unto one of another nation; but God hath shewed me that I should not call any man common or unclean.

29 Therefore came I unto you without gainsaying, as soon as I was sent for: I ask therefore for what intent ye have sent for me?

30 And Cornelius said, Four days ago I was fasting until this hour; and at the ninth hour I prayed in my house, and, behold, a man stood before me in bright clothing,

31 And said, Cornelius, thy prayer is heard, and thine alms are had in remembrance in the sight of God.

32 Send therefore to Joppa, and call hither Simon, whose surname is Peter; he is lodged in the house of one Simon a tanner by the sea side: who, when he cometh, shall speak unto thee.

33 Immediately therefore I sent to thee; and thou hast well done that thou art come. Now therefore are we all here present before God, to hear all things that are commanded thee of God.

34 Then Peter opened his mouth, and said, Of a truth I perceive that God is no respecter of persons:

35 But in every nation he that feareth him, and worketh righteousness, is accepted with him.

36 The word which God sent unto the children of Israel, preaching peace by Jesus Christ: (he is Lord of all:)

37 That word, I say, ye know, which was published throughout all Judæa, and began from Galilee, after the baptism which John

preached;

**38** How God anointed Jesus of Nazareth with the Holy Ghost and with power: who went about doing good, and healing all that were oppressed of the devil; for God was with him.

## LIFE NEED FOR TODAY'S LESSON

**AIM: You will discuss how people often show partiality to some and not others.**

## INTRODUCTION

### Tension in the Jewish Community

Jewish law was very specific about what Jews were to eat and how they were to conduct themselves. The dietary laws that Peter references are found in **Leviticus 11:1–47.** In their original form, these rules were meant to protect the people of Israel and set them apart as God's people. These laws and covenant agreements made it possible for sinful humanity to commune with God. However, through Christ's sacrifice, God had removed the barrier of sin between Himself and His people. Humanity could now commune with God through the acceptance of His Son Jesus Christ (**Romans 3:21–26**). This transition from law to grace through Christ created friction between Jewish Christians who still held to their Jewish culture and the new Gentile believers who hadn't converted to Judaism. Some Jewish believers expected that non-Jewish believers would fully convert to Judaism, taking on all Jewish customs and practices, including circumcision. This tension not only threatened the spread of the Gospel to Gentiles, but also the unity and potency of the Christian church.

Philip's encounter with an Ethiopian eunuch is recorded earlier in **Acts 8:26–38.** Similarly, salvation is given to the Ethiopian man based on his acceptance of Christ, not his cultural background. While this instance occurred in relative isolation, Peter's later interactions with Cornelius would be publicly known. This would represent a deep challenge to the beliefs of Jewish Christians, but it would also be an opportunity for them to finally understand God's will for the Gentiles.

## BIBLE LEARNING

**AIM: You will learn that Peter took risks and shared the Good News of Christ outside of the Jewish community.**

## I. PETER MEETS CORNELIUS
(Acts 10:24–26)

Peter, being obedient to the prompting of the Lord, has agreed to travel with Cornelius' men to Caesarea. Cornelius, apparently certain of Peter's arrival, has gathered friends and family to hear what Peter will share with them once he arrives. Cornelius' actions are indicative of his trust and belief in what God has instructed him to do. Not only does Cornelius do what he is instructed by sending men to find Peter, he expectantly looks forward to what God will do when Peter arrives.

Cornelius' response to Peter's arrival is to worship him. Peter quickly asks Cornelius to stop worshiping him and stand. Peter was already taking a risk by entering into the home of a Gentile, something forbidden by Jewish culture. It was important for Jews to avoid any appearance of idolatry, which included entering into the home of idolaters. Cornelius' worship of Peter would have been of immediate concern because it might have appeared to others that Peter was engaging in idolatry.

### Acts 10:24–38

**24 And the morrow after they entered into Caesarea. And Cornelius waited for them, and he had called together his kinsmen and near friends. 25 And as Peter was coming in, Cornelius met him, and fell down at his feet,**

and worshipped him. 26 But Peter took him up, saying, Stand up; I myself also am a man.

Peter enters into Caesarea after Cornelius dispatches a group to request Peter's presence in their home. Peter was accompanied by some disciples from Joppa on this journey. This would prove valuable as they would be eyewitnesses to what happened during Peter's preaching. Cornelius, seeing the gravity and importance of the occasion, invites his kinsmen and his close friends into his house.

Cornelius is struck with awe at Peter's visit. From this, we can infer that Cornelius believed Peter to be a servant of Jesus thinking that Peter is able to impart salvation. As a Greek Gentile who was steeped in paganism, the centurion offers him the required obeisance as a semidivine son of God who had supernatural powers. Cornelius' reaction is ingrained and reflexive. Peter refuses this worship and tells him to stand up because he was not a god, but a man.

## II. PETER SPEAKS TO CORNELIUS' GUESTS (vv. 27–29)

Upon entering Cornelius' home, Peter becomes aware that Cornelius has invited his friends and household to hear Peter. He explains his decision to accept Cornelius' invitation despite potential purity issues for entering a Gentile's home. He alludes to the vision he saw (**Acts 10:11–16**), sharing that he now understands that he is to no longer consider Gentiles unclean or impure. Consider how it must have felt for Cornelius and his friends to hear Peter, a devout Jew, tell them that he would no longer consider them impure because they are not Jewish like him. Furthermore, it was the God whom he serves that had shown him this truth.

27 And as he talked with him, he went in, and found many that were come together. 28 And he said unto them, Ye know how that it is an unlawful thing for a man that is a Jew to keep company, or come unto one of another nation; but God hath shewed me that I should not call any man common or unclean. 29 Therefore came I unto you without gainsaying, as soon as I was sent for: I ask therefore for what intent ye have sent for me?

Peter talks to Cornelius as they walk into the home. When he sees all the people gathered together, he sees an opportunity to express what God has revealed to him. He reminds them of how his presence there is unlawful (Gk. *athemitos*, **ah-THEH-mee-tos**), or contrary to accepted morality or social convention. In the Jewish context, it means forbidden and disgusting. Peter states that it is contrary to Jewish law for him to "keep company" with (Gk. *kollao*, **ko-LAH-oh**) or join together with a Gentile or enter a Gentile's home. Such practices were not prohibited by Jewish law. Instead, Peter is echoing a common Gentile perception at the time which developed out of table fellowship issues which caused some Jews to avoid eating with Gentiles because certain foods were prohibited in the Mosaic laws. Cornelius and his Gentile associates would have been surprised that Peter was willing to come into his home, and Peter explains that not only is it possible for them to fellowship together, but God has even told Peter that he should no longer think of anyone or anything as unclean (i.e., unacceptable to God without ritual purification). Peter says God has "shewed" (Gk. *deiknumi*, **DAKE-noo-mee**) him that he should not call any man common or unclean. The word for shewed means to establish the validity of something with an explanation or example. Here the explanation or example is the vision Peter receives on the rooftop of Simon the tanner (**Acts 10:9–16**). This vision is the basis for Peter's going to Cornelius' house without gainsaying (Gk. *anantirretos*, **ah-nahn-TEE-ray-tose**), or without objection.

## SEARCH THE SCRIPTURES

### QUESTION 1

The apostles traveled to _____ and were greeted by Cornelius.

### QUESTION 2

John states that people who fear and do what is right before God, are accepted by God. True or False?

## III. CORNELIUS' STORY (vv. 30–33)

It is now Cornelius' turn to explain why he has called for Peter. He describes the visit he received from the angel. Earlier in the chapter, Cornelius is described as being a "devout man" who "feared God" (vv. 1–2). The fact that he was fasting and praying when the Lord sent him the message is proof of this. His generosity to the poor has been noticed by God as well. Rather than explaining God's acceptance of Gentiles to Cornelius directly, the angel directs him to find Peter. In his obedience, Cornelius is used by God to help orchestrate His will for his family and Peter. God intends to minister to both parties in this experience. Cornelius now explains that they have been waiting expectantly for what God wishes to speak to them through Peter.

**30 And Cornelius said, Four days ago I was fasting until this hour; and at the ninth hour I prayed in my house, and, behold, a man stood before me in bright clothing, 31 And said, Cornelius, thy prayer is heard, and thine alms are had in remembrance in the sight of God. 32 Send therefore to Joppa, and call hither Simon, whose surname is Peter; he is lodged in the house of one Simon a tanner by the sea side: who, when he cometh, shall speak unto thee. 33 Immediately therefore I sent to thee; and thou hast well done that thou art come. Now therefore are we all here present before God, to hear all things that are commanded thee of God.**

Cornelius was a Roman centurion, or a captain in the army. Although the root word in centurion means "a hundred," a Roman centurion of this time would command eighty men. The Bible says he was a "devout man," which means he tried to be godly in his ways and gave God due reverence, evident by the fact that he positively influenced all those in his house, and he gave money to the poor while praying to God "alway" (**Acts 10:1–2**).

Cornelius recounted to Peter how God had given him a vision to send for Peter. It was around "the ninth hour," or 3 p.m., when Cornelius had a supernatural encounter. This mention of the ninth hour indicates Cornelius' adherence to the Jewish times of prayer, which corresponded with the morning and evening offerings in the temple. As a result of this Gentile man's efforts to know God, he was blessed with the vision, which would start a series of events leading to his salvation. The man who wore "bright clothing" was identified as an angel in the actual vision (**v. 3**). It is interesting that God spoke to both Peter and Cornelius in visions leading up to this fateful event.

The angel in the vision let Cornelius know that God had heard his prayer and his alms (Gk. *eleemosune*, **eh-leh-ay-moh-SOO-neigh**) were remembered (Gk. *mnaomai*, **muh-NAH-oh-my**), or God was mindful of them. The word for alms is literally compassion or pity. For some Jews in the Roman period, alms-giving was considered compatible with righteousness. Luke clearly intends to show that Cornelius was a righteous man and that God was answering the prayer of this righteous God-fearer. These God-fearers were Gentiles who were sympathetic to the Jewish religion. These were not full converts who were circumcised, but those who contributed to the synagogue and demonstrated piety.

Cornelius recounted his vision to Peter to explain why he had sent for him. The angel had instructed him, and therefore God had instructed him to do so. The omniscient God knew exactly where Peter was, just as He knows where all of our blessings are. The blessing that God had for Cornelius was that Peter would speak the gift of the Gospel message to him.

Peter was lodging with Simon the tanner (Gk. *burseus*, **bur-seh-OOS**). A tanner was a laborer who created leather from hides and skins by treating them with mineral lime and juices and leaves from various other plants. This leather was often used for making tents. The tabernacle coverings were made from the skins of rams or goats and were more than likely created by tanners (**Exodus 25:5, 26:14, 35:7, 23, 36:19**). Tanners were despised in Jewish culture. They were not allowed to go to the temple during pilgrimage season, and had their own synagogues because of the bad odor created by the animal hides. Even in Levirate marriage, the Mishnah or oral law allowed for the wife of the deceased brother of a tanner to remain a widow by saying "I could endure your brother, but I cannot endure you." Due to the odors, tanners were required to do their work outside the gates of the city or by the coast.

Cornelius thanked Peter for coming, but what he did not know was that God gave Peter a vision just before Cornelius's messengers arrived. In Peter's vision, God dealt with his feelings of prejudice toward Gentiles, while telling him to go with Cornelius' messengers (**Acts 10:9-20**). The mighty providence of God works everything out. God can weave a tapestry of people and events in our lives which appear to be unrelated or are totally unknown to us. Then, when the time is right, God will pull all the pieces together so that we are blessed with something He has been preparing for us for some time. Cornelius showed his love for his household by having everyone gathered to hear Peter's words. His example shows that we should not be selfish with God's Word of salvation. We should see that all of our relatives and friends get to hear it, whether from us or someone else. We owe it to those we love to give them a chance to hear the Gospel and receive the gift of salvation through Jesus Christ our Lord.

## IV. PETER DELIVERS THE GOSPEL (vv. 34–38)

At this point, it all becomes clear to Peter what God was doing and what he was to preach to Cornelius' people. Gentile uncleanness would no longer be a barrier to fellowship between Gentile and Jewish believers. God does not view Gentiles as unclean nor withhold fellowship from Gentiles on account of their racial and religious heritage, and neither should the Jewish people. They only need fear God and do what is right. Again, consider the impact of hearing Peter speak these words to the Gentile audience in Cornelius' home.

**34 Then Peter opened his mouth, and said, Of a truth I perceive that God is no respecter of persons. 35 But in every nation he that feareth him, and worketh righteousness, is accepted with him. 36 The word which God sent unto the children of Israel, preaching peace by Jesus Christ: (he is Lord of all:) 37 That word, I say, ye know, which was published throughout all Judea, and began from Galilee, after the baptism which John preached; 38 How God anointed Jesus of Nazareth with the Holy Ghost and with power: who went about doing good, and healing all that were oppressed of the devil; for God was with Him.**

Peter knew why he was there, so he went right to work. He began by acknowledging the truth that God had shown him in his own vision: "God is no respecter of persons." The phrase "respecter of persons" (Gk. *prosopolemptes*, **pro-so-po-LAYMP-tase**) is actually a single compound word in Greek that can mean "accepter of people." In this context it can be translated as "one who discriminates."

Peter lays out the foundation of his message: God is not one who discriminates.

In the event at Cornelius' house, God was using a formerly prejudiced Peter to initiate opening up the invitation of the Gospel to Gentiles everywhere. No matter what nationality, God accepts the one who "feareth" (Gk. *phobeo*, **fo-BEH-oh**) Him, which means showing Him deference and reverence. He also accepts the one who "worketh" (Gk. *ergazomai*, **er-GOD-zo-my**) righteousness, which is to "produce" righteousness. This is an appropriate description of Cornelius as a God-fearer who prayed and gave alms regularly.

Peter began to lay out the chronological progression of the Gospel. He told his audience that God started by sending His Word to the Children of Israel. This Word was the preaching of peace (Gk. *eirene*, **ay-RAY-nay**) by Jesus Christ. Peter shows how the Gospel was first given to Israel and was expected, according to Old Testament prophecy, to bring peace (**Isaiah 52:7**). Later in Isaiah, peace would be proclaimed to everyone far and near which includes Gentiles as well as the Jews (**Isaiah 57:19**). Peter also says that Jesus is "Lord of all," reinforcing the truth of God being "no respecter of persons" (**v. 34**).

Peter encouraged them by saying that they already knew about some aspects of the message, which had spread to areas beyond Jerusalem. The word for published (Gk. *ginomai*, **GIH-no-my**) here is not in the sense of a publishing a book, but can mean to arise in history or come on the stage (cf. John 1:4). Judea was usually the name of the southern region of Palestine. In this case, it is a term for the whole of the Roman province of Judea. He indicated that the ministry of Jesus began in Galilee after His baptism by John the Baptist. John preached a message of water baptism and repentance from sin (**Mark 1:4**).

Peter then told his audience about the earthly ministry of Jesus. He said that Jesus was "anointed with the Holy Ghost and with power" (**Matthew 3:16**). Then Jesus did good and miraculous works, such as healing people with all sorts of ailments (cf. **Matthew 8:2–3, 9:20–22, 12:10–13; John 11:43–44**). The word for "doing good" can mean more than just being a "do-gooder"; it can specifically refer to rulers and deities who benefit their subjects. By using the phrase "God was with him," Peter connects Jesus to Old Testament figures such as Joseph, David, and Nehemiah (**Genesis 39:3, 23, 1 Samuel 18:12; Nehemiah 1:8**). These figures enjoyed the approval of God and His blessing on their endeavors. God Himself expressed that He was with Jesus, saying, "This is my beloved Son, in whom I am well pleased; hear ye him" (**Matthew 17:5**). Through this description, Peter establishes the uniqueness of Jesus' life and ministry and how the God who accepts all endorsed His ministry.

## SEARCH THE SCRIPTURES

### QUESTION 3
Why was it considered against Jewish law for Peter to go into the house of Cornelius (**NIV, v. 28**)?

### QUESTION 4
What caused Peter to realize that God does not show favoritism (**NIV, v. 34**)?

## BIBLE APPLICATION

**AIM: You will understand that sharing the Gospel is challenging.**

Jewish and Gentile believers were learning that salvation was based on their acceptance of Christ, not cultural heritage or outward actions. Today, despite having freely received the acceptance and love of God through Jesus Christ, it is easy for us to slip into thinking that we have somehow done (or can continue doing) things that warrant God's approval. This quickly results in judging others based on how well they live up to a human standard of righteousness. However, when we remember that we are only accepted by God's grace through Jesus Christ, we can extend grace, love, and acceptance to those around us (**Romans 5:15–17**).

## STUDENT'S RESPONSES

**AIM: You will know that God expects believers to extend a welcome to all.**

Peter took a risk by going to Cornelius' home and ministering to his household. Are there any ways in which God is asking you to take a risk to reach out to someone? Prayerfully consider stepping out and allowing the Holy Spirit to guide you in ministering to that person.

## PRAYER

Dear Gracious God, Your love is gracious and everlasting. Your Word is loving and encouraging for us even when others speak against You. Bless us and keep us in Your perfect care. In the Name of Jesus, we pray. Amen.

## HOW TO SAY IT

Caesarea.     **SEE**-se-ree-uh.

Joppa.     **JAH**-puh.

## PREPARE FOR NEXT SUNDAY

Read **Acts 11:1–18** and "Trusting the Spirit."

## DAILY HOME BIBLE READINGS

### MONDAY
God's Love Prevails
(Romans 8:31–39)

### TUESDAY
Peter Takes a Risk
(Matthew 14:22–33)

### WEDNESDAY
Lord of the Sabbath
(Matthew 12:1–8)

### THURSDAY
Peter is Stretched
(Acts 10:1–16)

### FRIDAY
Peter Follows Through
(Acts 10:17–23)

### SATURDAY
God is For All
(Acts 10:39–48)

### SUNDAY
Peter Takes Another Risk
(Acts 10:24–38)

**Sources:**

Alexander, David, and Pat Alexander. *Zondervan Handbook to the Bible*. Grand Rapids, MI: Zondervan, 1999. 649.

Barker, Kenneth L. and Kohlenberger III, John R., eds. *The Expositor's Bible Commentary—Abridged Edition: New Testament*. Grand Rapids, MI: Zondervan, 1994. 441.

Burge, Gary M. and Hill, Andrew E. eds. *Baker Illustrated Bible Commentary*. Grand Rapids, MI: Baker Books, 2012. 1187.

Carson, D. A., R. T. France, J. A. Motyer, G. J. Wenham, Eds. *New Bible Commentary*. Downers Grove, IL: InterVarsity Press, 1994. 1082.

Elwell, Walter A. ed. *Baker Commentary on the Bible*. Grand Rapids, MI: Baker Books, 1989. 898-899.

Elwell, Walter A. and Yarbrough, Robert W. *Encountering the New Testament: A Historical and Theological Survey*. Grand Rapids, MI: Baker Books, 1998. 227.

Kaiser, Walter C. Jr., and Garrett, Duane. *NIV Archaeological Study Bible*. Grand Rapids, MI: Zondervan, 2005. 1784, 1786.

Keener, Craig S. *The IVP Bible Background Commentary: New Testament*. Downers Grove, IL: InterVarsity Press, 1993. 352-353.

Orr, James, ed. "Tanner." *International Standard Bible Encyclopedia*. Electronic Edition. Omaha, NE: Quickverse, 1998.

Richards, Lawrence O. ed. "Tanning." *Richards Complete Bible Dictionary*. Iowa Falls, IA: World Bible Publishers, 2002.

Thayer, Joseph. "anantirrhetos." *Thayer's Greek Definitions*. 3rd ed. Electronic Edition, Quickverse. El Cajon, CA: Institute for Creation Research, 1999.

Thayer, Joseph. "prosopoleptes." *Thayer's Greek Definitions*. 3rd ed. Electronic Edition, Quickverse. El Cajon, CA: Institute for Creation Research, 1999.

# TRUSTING THE SPIRIT

**BIBLE BASIS:** ACTS 11:1–18

**BIBLE TRUTH:** Peter's testimony to the power of the Holy Spirit converting Gentiles increased the Jerusalem's church support of Peter.

**MEMORY VERSE:** "Forasmuch then as God gave them the like gift as he did unto us, who believed on the Lord Jesus Christ; what was I,

that I could withstand God?" (Acts 11:17).

**LESSON AIM:** By the end of the lesson, we will LEARN that Peter's preaching to the Gentiles was affirmed by the believers in Jerusalem; FEEL comfortable with reaching out to different peoples; and IDENTIFY Christian Scriptures that include all in the Body of Christ.

## LESSON SCRIPTURE

### ACTS 11:1–18, KJV

1 And the apostles and brethren that were in Judaea heard that the Gentiles had also received the word of God.

2 And when Peter was come up to Jerusalem, they that were of the circumcision contended with him,

3 Saying, Thou wentest in to men uncircumcised, and didst eat with them.

4 But Peter rehearsed the matter from the beginning, and expounded it by order unto them, saying,

5 I was in the city of Joppa praying: and in a trance I saw a vision, A certain vessel descend, as it had been a great sheet, let down from heaven by four corners; and it came even to me:

6 Upon the which when I had fastened mine eyes, I considered, and saw fourfooted beasts of the earth, and wild beasts, and creeping things, and fowls of the air.

7 And I heard a voice saying unto me, Arise, Peter; slay and eat.

8 But I said, Not so, Lord: for nothing

common or unclean hath at any time entered into my mouth.

9 But the voice answered me again from heaven, What God hath cleansed, that call not thou common.

10 And this was done three times: and all were drawn up again into heaven.

11 And, behold, immediately there were three men already come unto the house where I was, sent from Caesarea unto me.

12 And the Spirit bade me go with them, nothing doubting. Moreover these six brethren accompanied me, and we entered into the man's house:

13 And he shewed us how he had seen an angel in his house, which stood and said unto him, Send men to Joppa, and call for Simon, whose surname is Peter;

14 Who shall tell thee words, whereby thou and all thy house shall be saved.

15 And as I began to speak, the Holy Ghost fell on them, as on us at the beginning.

16 Then remembered I the word of the Lord, how that he said, John indeed baptized with

water; but ye shall be baptized with the Holy Ghost.

**17** Forasmuch then as God gave them the like gift as he did unto us, who believed on the Lord Jesus Christ; what was I, that I could withstand God?

**18** When they heard these things, they held their peace, and glorified God, saying, Then hath God also to the Gentiles granted repentance unto life.

## LIFE NEED FOR TODAY'S LESSON

**AIM: You will see how people who act outside of the norm are required to justify their actions.**

## INTRODUCTION

### God Speaks to Peter

Jesus gave the early church a commission to expand beyond Jerusalem and Judea in preaching the Gospel (**Acts 1:8**). We do not know whether the disciples understood this as a commission to preach specifically to the Gentiles or only to the Jews of the Diaspora. Up until the time of the first persecution following the martyrdom of Stephen, the Gospel was restricted to the Jewish people.

The persecution scattered the believers and many of the Greek-speaking Jews began to preach the Gospel everywhere they went (**Acts 8:4**). Philip began to preach in Samaria and this was the first significant advance of the Gospel into non-Jewish territory (**Acts 8:5–12**). After the conversion of Saul, the churches enjoyed a relative peace (**Acts 9:31**).

## BIBLE LEARNING

**AIM: You will explore how the church in Jerusalem supported Peter's preaching and conversions of the Gentiles.**

## I. PETER IS CHALLENGED (Acts 11:1–3)

Peter most likely knew that he would be expected to account for his actions in Caesarea. By the time he returns to Jerusalem, word has already spread of his encounter with Cornelius and his family. The believers referred to as "of the circumcision" in **verse 2** are Christian Jews who strongly identified with their Jewish heritage. It was disturbing to them that Peter had seemingly set aside his Jewish piety. Peter had eaten with Gentiles, clearly violating Kosher law. From the perspective of first century Jews, this placed Peter in the company of idolaters and people considered unclean because they did not adhere to Jewish dietary restrictions. Furthermore, sharing a meal was a sign of intimate fellowship and acceptance in the Jewish culture. God calls us to accept people not just in our heads but to show our acceptance and connect with them on a personal level.

## Acts 11:1–18

**1 And the apostles and brethren that were in Judaea heard that the Gentiles had also received the word of God. 2 And when Peter was come up to Jerusalem, they that were of the circumcision contended with him, 3 Saying, Thou wentest in to men uncircumcised, and didst eat with them.**

The news concerning the reception of the Gentiles into the Christian fellowship, marked by the conversion of Cornelius, has reached Jerusalem. The conversion of Cornelius was a landmark in the history of the Gospel's advance from its strictly Jewish beginnings to its saturation of the Roman Empire. It was a proof that the sovereign God was not confined to the traditional forms of Judaism and could bring a Gentile directly into relationship with Himself through Jesus Christ apart from any prior commitment to distinctive Jewish beliefs or lifestyle. However, Peter's actions were an affront to the traditions and prejudices of the Jewish Christians. The Jerusalem council summoned him to give an account of all that had transpired. He needed to provide answers to those who might have been unsettled by the episode, probably thinking that he had taken a liberal attitude toward the law. It says that those who were "of the circumcision" (Gk. *peritome*, **peh-ree-toh-MAY**), or circumcised Jews, contended (Gk. *diakrino*, **dee-ah-KREE-no**) or disputed with Peter. He was attacked not for preaching to the "uncircumcised" Gentiles or their being baptized, but for his social relations with them. Peter's eating with the Gentiles showed his acceptance of them as fellow Christians, and they were still uncircumcised (**v. 3**). Peter defends his actions by narrating how God led him to Cornelius and how the Spirit fell on Cornelius and his household.

## II. PETER SHARES HIS VISION (vv. 4–10)

Peter responds to his critics by first citing his experience in Joppa. While in a trance, he had received the unsettling directive that he should kill and eat animals that Jews are clearly forbidden to eat. The foods that Peter refers to as "common or unclean" (**Acts 11:8**) are described at length in **Leviticus 11**. Among these restrictions are very specific rules related to these animals. Only certain animals that walked on all fours were allowed to be eaten. Specific birds and insects, like the locust, were allowed, while most others were off limits. Peter's response to the Lord indicates that he is very aware of these restrictions. He explains that he has never once violated them and refuses to do so. Peter's protest is met with the correction that he is to no longer consider something unclean if God has declared it otherwise. Upon waking, Peter must have been somewhat confused by what he saw and heard. But he would eventually understand it completely. We can only understand God fully if we continue obeying His revelation.

**4 But Peter rehearsed the matter from the beginning, and expounded it by order unto them, saying, 5 I was in the city of Joppa praying: and in a trance I saw a vision, A certain vessel descend, as it had been a great sheet, let down from heaven by four corners; and it came even to me: 6 Upon the which when I had fastened mine eyes, I considered, and saw fourfooted beasts of the earth, and wild beasts, and creeping things, and fowls of the air 7 And I heard a voice saying unto me, Arise, Peter; slay and eat. 8 But I said, Not so, Lord: for nothing common or unclean hath at any time entered into my mouth. 9 But the voice answered me again from heaven, What God hath cleansed, that call not thou common. 10 And this was done three times: and all were drawn up again into heaven.**

Peter relates his vision by quickly leading them to the main issue—God's acceptance of the Gentiles. Peter begins with his own vision in **11:5–10**, which is a detailed retelling of **10:9–16**. In fact, that is the most extensive repetition in his report to Jerusalem. For Peter, it was the heart of the matter—there are no unclean people, and God accepts the Gentiles.

It all began with Peter on a rooftop in Joppa. This is where he experienced a vision (Gk. *horama*, **HO-rah-mah**), which is a sight divinely granted in a trance (Gk. *ekstasis*, **EK-sta-sees**) or ecstasy. A trance can be defined as a throwing of the mind out of its normal state. Although the person is awake, the mind is closed off from surrounding physical objects and fixed on the divine forms and things within a particular vision. When Peter was in the trance, he observed a sheet coming down out of heaven filled with all kinds of animals forbidden for Jews to eat, because they were not kosher. As the sheet was let down from heaven, a voice said, "Arise, Peter; slay and eat." Peter's response was that he had never eaten anything common (Gk. *koinos*, **koy-NOS**) or unclean (Gk. *akathartos*, **ah-KA-thar-tose**). *Koinos* is the term the Jews of that day used for anything common or eaten by anybody, i.e., the Gentiles. The word for unclean is also a general word for uncleansed and specifically for things that are Levitically unclean. In using both words, we see Peter explicitly stating his case: He has never eaten these animals and never intended to.

Next the voice says, "What God hath cleansed, that call not thou common." In other words, what was considered unclean, God has now cleansed. This was done three times. In Scripture when something happens three times, it is usually an indication of the thing being established by God, as in the case of Jonah being three days in the belly of the whale or the angels crying out "Holy, Holy, Holy" to God on the throne. This was significant, as Peter was being asked to do something that was in violation of everything he knew as a Jew. His core identity was being challenged in this vision and would be again further in the narrative.

## SEARCH THE SCRIPTURES

### QUESTION 1
In what city was Peter when God shared a vision with Peter (**v. 5**)?

### QUESTION 2
Describe the beasts that Peter saw in the vision (**v. 6**).

## III. PETER'S JOURNEY TO CAESAREA (vv. 11–14)

Peter immediately has the opportunity to begin acting on his new information. He obediently agrees to travel to Caesarea, but is still not fully aware of the significance of the Lord's message. His reservations about traveling with the Gentile men might have kept him in Joppa if it weren't for the Holy Spirit's reassurance (**v. 12**). Note that God's guidance factors heavily in Peter's retelling of the experience. His decision to travel to Caesarea wasn't based solely on his own desire; he was being obedient to God's direction.

The story moves ahead to Cornelius' retelling of his own experience in Caesarea. Again, Peter gives God the credit for orchestrating all these events. As Peter retells it, Cornelius is promised that based on the message that Peter would share, he and his entire household would be saved.

**11 And, behold, immediately there were three men already come unto the house where I was, sent from Caesarea unto me. 12 And the spirit bade me go with them, nothing doubting. Moreover these six brethren accompanied me, and we entered into the man's house: 13 And he shewed us how he had seen an angel in his house, which stood and said unto him, Send men to Joppa, and call for Simon, whose surname is Peter; 14 Who shall tell thee words, whereby thou and all thy house shall be saved. 15 And as I began to speak, the Holy Ghost fell on them, as on us at the beginning. 16 Then remembered I the word of the Lord, how that he said, John indeed baptized with water; but ye shall be baptized with the Holy Ghost. 17 Forasmuch then as God gave them the like gift as he did unto us, who believed on the Lord Jesus Christ; what was I, that I could withstand God? 18 When they heard these things, they held their peace, and glorified God, saying, Then hath God also to the Gentiles granted repentance unto life.**

**Verses 11–12** summarize the narrative of **10:17–25**, relating the arrival of the three messengers from Cornelius and Peter's accompanying them to Caesarea. The most significant difference from the earlier account is Peter's mention of six brothers from Joppa who accompanied him to Caesarea (**v. 12**). "These six" whom Peter brought to Jerusalem served as witnesses to what transpired in Cornelius's home (cf. **10:45**).

**Verses 13–14** summarize Cornelius' vision, how the angel instructed him to send to Joppa for Peter. **Verse 14** is more specific than any of the accounts of Cornelius' vision in Acts 10. Peter was to bring a message to Cornelius "through which [he] and all [his] household [would] be saved." This expansion elucidates Cornelius' eager anticipation of Peter's message in **10:33**. There is no need for Peter to summarize the sermon he gave Cornelius before the Jerusalem Christians, so he quickly moves to the coming of the Spirit on the Gentiles at the house (**v. 15**). Peter notes how the event interrupted his sermon and adds that the Spirit came upon them just "as on us at the beginning." This compares the episode at Cornelius' house to that on the day of Pentecost. Peter makes explicit here what was implicit in **10:46**. He continues to draw the comparison in **v. 16**, which harkens back to **Acts 1:5** and Jesus' prediction of a baptism with the Holy Spirit. Jesus' prediction was fulfilled for the apostles at Pentecost; for Cornelius and his fellow Gentiles, it was fulfilled with the coming of the Spirit at Cornelius's house. Certainly for Peter, it was a Gentile Pentecost. He could hardly make more explicit comparisons!

Peter concludes his report in Jerusalem (**vv. 17–18**) by reminding his hearers once again that God gave the gift of the Spirit to the Gentiles and added, "What was I, that I could withstand God," that is, "Who am I to think that I can oppose God?" Peter uses the same verb *koluo* (Gk. **ko-LOO-oh**) that he previously used in **10:47** to express the same idea of opposing God, to question whether it was appropriate for anyone to forbid or oppose the baptism of the Gentiles. For anyone to do so would be tantamount to opposing God, for His leading of Peter and Cornelius was beyond doubt. God intended to include the Gentiles in His people; He was clearly behind it.

The Jerusalem leaders quietly listened as Peter told his story. There is no sign that they interrupted him or distrusted his words. As they listened, they realized that they had been wrong. They seemed to be more eager to grasp truth than to defend their own positions, a timely lesson for any Christian, particularly leaders today. When Peter clearly showed that God was bigger than their opinions, they let their prejudices go. After

Peter finished, the conservative Jerusalem group had no further objections (**v. 18**). In the face of the evidence that Peter provided, his critics had nothing more to say. They accepted what had happened, concluding that God had granted even the Gentiles repentance, reaching out to those to whom they would not have reached out and in a manner they never would have approved. Silence quickly gave way to praise of God in His triumphant advance of the Gospel. God had granted "repentance unto life" to the Gentiles. They rejoiced in the results of Peter's action, which previously they had criticized.

## IV. PETER'S CHALLENGERS ARE CONVINCED (vv. 15–18)

The circumcised believers that Peter is speaking to were about to hear something that would take them all by surprise. Peter shares the Gospel with Cornelius and his household, and at that point, the Holy Spirit fell on everyone there. Peter draws the connection between this event at Cornelius' home and the event they had all experienced on the Day of Pentecost (**Acts 2:1–13**). In pouring out the Holy Spirit on these Gentile believers just as He had on the apostles, God has shown that He views them in the same way. Despite their cultural differences, the gift of the Holy Spirit was an experience that they shared in common. Furthermore, Peter points out the words of Christ regarding baptism with the Holy Spirit: "John indeed baptized with water; but ye shall be baptized with the Holy Ghost" (**Acts 11:16**). Along with circumcision, ritual cleansing was also used as an indication of conversion to Judaism. By referring to the Gentile experience as a baptism with the Holy Spirit, Peter indicates that God now sees them as converted.

Peter completes his argument by once again explaining that God's will was at work in all of these events. To oppose the course of events that played out would have been to oppose God.

## SEARCH THE SCRIPTURES

### QUESTION 3
How did the Holy Spirit interact with the Gentiles (**v. 15**)?

### QUESTION 4
Peter challenged the conservative Jerusalem group to answer what question?

## BIBLE APPLICATION

**AIM: You will learn that God desires that believers would communicate His love toward others regardless of their cultural or religious backgrounds.**

Peter and the Jewish Christians had to overcome biases that developed out of their initial desire to do what was right. What were initially legitimate convictions about how to please God had turned into shows of favoritism and bigotry. This same dynamic plays itself out in today's Christian church. Often, one group's differing religious views become a reason they are mistrusted or mistreated by other believers. Regardless of our differing views, we are all one body in Christ (**1 Corinthians 12:12–13**).

## STUDENT'S RESPONSES

**AIM: You will learn that you should trust the Holy Spirit to guide you as you witness to others about Christ.**

Do you see yourself as someone who is welcoming to others despite significant outward differences? If so, how might you be able to encourage your friends to see people the way God sees them?

Do you sometimes feel pressure to treat people differently because they don't share your beliefs or background? We can ask God to give us the strength and guidance of the Holy Spirit to help us accept others and show Christ's love.

## PRAYER

Lord, we adore You and worship You. The Holy Spirit comforts us and allows us to share the joy of Jesus with family, friends, and those we do not know. Your gentle care is refreshing and good news for us all. In the Name of Jesus, we pray. Amen.

## HOW TO SAY IT

Judaea.        joo-DEE-uh.

Expounded.     eks-POWN-ded.

## PREPARE FOR NEXT SUNDAY

Read **Acts 12:1–11** and "Prayer Works!"

### DAILY HOME BIBLE READINGS

**MONDAY**
A Light to the Nations
(Acts 10:24–38)

**TUESDAY**
Water for Everyone
(John 4:3–14)

**WEDNESDAY**
Your Gentle Defense
(1 Peter 3:13–18)

**THURSDAY**
Strangers Become Heaven's Citizens
(Ephesians 2:11–22)

**FRIDAY**
Good News to Great Joy
(Acts 8:4–8)

**SATURDAY**
Called Christians
(Acts 10:19–26)

## SUNDAY
### Trusting the Spirit
### (Acts 11:1–18)

**Sources:**

Arrington, French L. *The Acts of the Apostles: An Introduction and Commentary.* Peabody, Mass.: Hendrickson, 1988.

Barker, Kenneth L. and Kohlenberger III, John R., eds. *The Expositor's Bible Commentary–Abridged Edition: New Testament.* Grand Rapids, MI: Zondervan, 1994. 442-443.

Keener, Craig S. *The IVP Bible Background Commentary: New Testament.* Downers Grove, IL: InterVarsity Press, 1993. 354.

Longenecker, Richard N. "Acts," in *The Expositor's Bible Commentary: Luke–Acts (Revised Edition),* ed. Tremper Longman III and David E. Garland, vol. 10. Grand Rapids, MI: Zondervan, 2007, 884.

Marshall, I Howard. *The Acts of the Apostles: An Introduction and Commentary.* The Tyndale New Testament Commentaries. Grand Rapids, Mich.: W.B. Eerdmans Pub. Co., 1980.

Polhill, John B. *Acts, vol. 26.* The New American Commentary. Nashville: Broadman & Holman Publishers, 1995.

## COMMENTS / NOTES:

# PRAYER WORKS!

**BIBLE BASIS:** ACTS 12:1–11

**BIBLE TRUTH:** The fervent prayer of the church in Acts and the work of an angel provided Peter's deliverance.

**MEMORY VERSE:** "Peter therefore was kept in prison: but prayer was made without ceasing of the church unto God for him" (Acts 12:5).

**LESSON AIM:** By the end of the lesson, we will: EXPLORE the story of Peter's deliverance from prison; RECOGNIZE and appreciate the power of prayer in difficult circumstances; and COMMIT to praying for those whose witness puts them in life-threatening or difficult situations.

## LESSON SCRIPTURE

### ACTS 12:1–11, KJV

1 Now about that time Herod the king stretched forth his hands to vex certain of the church.

2 And he killed James the brother of John with the sword.

3 And because he saw it pleased the Jews, he proceeded further to take Peter also. (Then were the days of unleavened bread.)

4 And when he had apprehended him, he put him in prison, and delivered him to four quaternions of soldiers to keep him; intending after Easter to bring him forth to the people.

5 Peter therefore was kept in prison: but prayer was made without ceasing of the church unto God for him.

6 And when Herod would have brought him forth, the same night Peter was sleeping between two soldiers, bound with two chains: and the keepers before the door kept the prison.

7 And, behold, the angel of the Lord came upon him, and a light shined in the prison: and he smote Peter on the side, and raised him up, saying, Arise up quickly. And his chains fell off from his hands.

8 And the angel said unto him, Gird thyself, and bind on thy sandals. And so he did. And he saith unto him, Cast thy garment about thee, and follow me.

9 And he went out, and followed him; and wist not that it was true which was done by the angel; but thought he saw a vision.

10 When they were past the first and the second ward, they came unto the iron gate that leadeth unto the city; which opened to them of his own accord: and they went out, and passed on through one street; and forthwith the angel departed from him.

11 And when Peter was come to himself, he said, Now I know of a surety, that the Lord hath sent his angel, and hath delivered me out of the hand of Herod, and from all the expectation of the people of the Jews.

## LIFE NEED FOR TODAY'S LESSON

**AIM: You are reminded that in the midst of perilous life situations, deliverance sometimes appears to come through miraculous means.**

# INTRODUCTION

## God's People and Church Persecuted

God's people have always been persecuted or hunted down throughout the centuries. During the time of the Old Testament, this persecution was directed toward many of the Old Testament prophets. Elijah was an enemy of the state during the wicked reign of Ahab (**1 Kings 19:1–3**). Jeremiah was thrown in prison by King Zedekiah (**Jeremiah 32:1–5**). Rabbinical sources state that Isaiah was sawed in half during the reign of King Manasseh. Regardless of whether they escaped or lost their lives, these prophets depended on and trusted in God.

The early church faced waves of persecution. This began with the martydom of Stephen and was led by Saul the Pharisee. Once Saul was converted to Christ, the churches had rest from persecution and gained a short season of peace. Soon, during a time of famine, the church was targeted by King Herod Agrippa, who was pro-Pharisee and beloved by the Jewish establishment.

# BIBLE LEARNING

**AIM: You will know that believers should pray together and expect God to answer.**

# I. PUNISHED FOR PREACHING (Acts 12:1–3)

Peter seems to have been made for tough times, considering the various challenges he experienced during and since his days walking with Jesus. He was once personally vexed by the crowing rooster when he realized he had denied Jesus just before the crucifixion (**John 18:15–27**). Now, Peter finds himself the victim of a vengeful and jealous king seeking to kill him as an example to deter believers in Christ. The persecution of the early church came largely from two forces: the imperial Roman government and the established Jewish leadership (cf. **Acts 9:1–2**). Referred to as "Herod," the king is Herod Agrippa, who like many similar rulers was known for his violent acts toward his enemies. Killing James "with the sword" is generally understood to be a beheading (**v. 2**). This was also intended to be Peter's fate. Beheading is a severe and immediate form of capital punishment, symbolizing silencing of offender. Herod's desire to "vex" or torment the church by punishing its leaders was a ploy to keep followers in line by brutish example.

# Acts 12:1–11

**1 Now about that time Herod the king stretched forth his hands to vex certain of the church. 2 And he killed James the brother of John with the sword. 3 And because he saw it pleased the Jews, he proceeded further to take Peter also. (Then were the days of unleavened bread.)**

The "time" referred to is during a famine in Judea (**Acts 11:28**). This is now the third of four Herods to enter the Luke-Acts narrative. The first was Herod the Great, who reigned during the priesthood of Zacharias (**Luke 1:5**). The second was Herod Antipas, who shadowed Jesus' ministry, death, and resurrection (**Luke 9:7–9; 23:7–15**). This "Herod the king" in **Acts 12:1** is Herod Agrippa I, the grandson of Herod the Great and the father of Herod Agrippa II (**Acts 25:13–26**). Herod Agrippa I had been brought up in Rome, where he made many influential friends—among whom were Gaius Caligula and Claudius. When Caligula became emperor (AD 37–41), he granted Herod the tetrarchies ruled by Philip and Lysanius (**Luke 3:1**). Later he added the tetrarchy of Herod Antipas to Herod Agrippa's possessions. After Caligula's assassination, Herod helped Claudius receive confirmation from the Roman senate as emperor. The new emperor added Judea and Samaria to Herod's kingdom. So from AD 41 to the time of his death in AD 44, Herod Agrippa I ruled over a reassembled kingdom the same size as his grandfather, Herod the Great. He was as loved by the Jewish establishment as his grandfather was hated.

Herod Agrippa was committed to maintaining a peace favorable to Rome—a policy called "Pax Romana." Therefore, he supported the religious establishment and was hostile toward all who saw things differently. Because he saw Jewish Christians as disruptive, he sought to suppress them. To this end, he arrested some of Jesus' followers and had James executed. This James was one of the first followers of Jesus (**Luke 5:10**) and was one of the Twelve (**Luke 6:14–16**). He, along with his brother John (son of Zebedee) and Peter were close friends with Jesus (**Luke 8:51, 9:28**). He was often called James the Great to distinguish him from James the son of Alphaeus (**Acts 1:13**). He was also not to be confused with James, the half-brother of Jesus (**Galatians 1:19**). The death of James signaled the end of the short period of tranquility enjoyed by the Jerusalem leadership after Saul's conversion (**Acts 9:31**).

Upon seeing that his action pleased the Jews, Herod Agrippa I had Peter arrested to preserve the status quo. The reason "it pleased the Jews" may also lie in the means of James' execution. In the Talmud, the rabbis considered beheading the most shameful of all deaths, reserved for those who had no share in the world to come. The execution of James was therefore a gesture of solidarity on Herod's part with the Jewish majority, a statement that he regarded Jesus' followers as apostates and agitators. Luke parenthetically told his readers that these "were the days of unleavened bread." Although the celebration of the feast began with the Passover meal on 14 Nisan (the first month of the Jewish calendar), the "days of unleavened bread" continued for seven days more (**Exodus 12:3–20, 23:15, 34:18**). The reader is expected to make the connection between this arrest and that of Jesus, which also occurred at Passover.

## SEARCH THE SCRIPTURES

### QUESTION 1
James was a significant church leader. How was James killed?

## II. BOXED IN (vv. 4–6)

Peter's crime of preaching could not have been so severe as to warrant the intensity of his imprisonment, yet he is held like one sentenced for a capital crime. He is guarded by a group of four soldiers who completely surround Peter at all times. Two are on watch and the other two are chained to him (**v. 6**). In essence, being surrounded on four sides, Peter was boxed in. Not only was he relegated to the enclosed box of the prison cell, but with round-the-clock guards, and two of them physically bound to him, there was absolutely no way to escape.

In light of the lesson's theme, Peter's circumstances are clearly at such a critical point that only prayer—and a divine intervention—could bring about a change. Prayer is described as offering, or an address to God. That the church prayed "without ceasing" underscores the importance of communicating with God even more fervently when other resources are not available. Addressing the king through political appeal is not mentioned. A rescue or demand for a proper trial is not attempted. There is only the church instituting constant and fervent prayer, a concept that remains today (**1 Thessalonians 5:17**). If indeed a believer is found to be in an impossible situation, there is no other remedy than to call upon the King of Kings.

**4 And when he had apprehended him, he put him in prison, and delivered him to four quaternions of soldiers to keep him; intending after Easter to bring him forth to the people. 5 Peter therefore was kept in prison: but prayer was made without ceasing**

of the church unto God for him. 6 And when Herod would have brought him forth, the same night Peter was sleeping between two soldiers, bound with two chains: and the keepers before the door kept the prison.

The delay functions in the narrative to build tension and allows the reader to see the activity of the church working against that of Herod. Overall, the action stands in contrast to the summary execution of James by "the sword" in **verse 2**. We can see the importance of this trial in the eyes of Herod as Peter is guarded by four quaternions, or sixteen soldiers.

While Peter was in prison, the believers were continually praying to God for him. Throughout Acts, the church is portrayed as a praying community (**Acts 1:14, 24; 2:42; 4:24–30; 13:3**). The adverbial phrase "without ceasing" (Gk. *ektenes*, **ek-teh-OSE**) denotes eagerness and earnestness. It is from a verb that means to stretch out the hand, implying an attitude of not relaxing until a thing is accomplished. The community's prayer is contrasted with Peter's powerlessness to escape.

Herod may have heard of Peter and John's earlier escape and decided to fortify security measures (**Acts 5:17–20**). Luke takes time to break down the duties of one quaternion. The custom with such squads was to have four men on duty at a time, in four revolving watches. Here two slept next to Peter and one was at each of the two guard posts (**v. 10**). These elaborate security measures heighten the wonder of the escape.

## III. DIVINE DELIVERANCE (vv. 7–10)

It is difficult to imagine how Peter could possibly sleep (**v. 6**) or get any rest. As he faces his death sentence, as well as being physically chained to two guards, he is as tightly confined as possible. Yet God uses sleep as a method of veiling His actions while enforcing His will. Peter has no time to ask questions or to confirm the angel's identity or purpose;

he is only able to follow instructions to end the present dilemma (**v. 8**). Whether through a vision or an angel or ghost, God hears the prayers of His people and delivers them out of their trials.

7 And, behold, the angel of the Lord came upon him, and a light shined in the prison: and he smote Peter on the side, and raised him up, saying, Arise up quickly. And his chains fell off from his hands. 8 And the angel said unto him, Gird thyself, and bind on thy sandals. And so he did. And he saith unto him, Cast thy garment about thee, and follow me. 9 And he went out, and followed him; and wist not that it was true which was done by the angel; but thought he saw a vision. 10 When they were past the first and the second ward, they came unto the iron gate that leadeth unto the city; which opened to them of his own accord: and they went out, and passed on through one street; and forthwith the angel departed from him.

The angel appears to Peter and instructs him to get up. These messengers from God played an important role through substantial portions of the books of Luke and Acts (**Luke 1:11, 26; 2:9, 13; Acts 8:26; 27:23**). Together, the use of the words "behold" (Gk. *idou*, **ee-DOO**) and "came upon" (Gk. *ephistemi*, **eh-FEES-tay-me**) gives the sense of a sudden and startling appearance (cf. Luke 2:9). As with the appearance to Saul, "light" (Gk. *phos*, **FOCE**) was a sign of heavenly presence (**Acts 9:3; 22:6, 9–11**).

Peter followed the instructions of the angel, although he believed it was a vision. It is important to note that Peter gets fully dressed. He puts on his shoes and belt as well as his outer garment or coat. This indicates it was not a swift escape made with human effort, but the work of God. The verb "thought" (Gk. *dokeo*, **doh-keh-OH**) is in the imperfect active tense, which means that while the escape was taking place, he kept on thinking and being confused about whether he was in a vision. It is only after the angel departs that Peter realizes the escape is real.

## IV. THE DOORS OF THE CHURCH ARE OPEN (vv. 11–12)

Peter "came to himself." He collected his thoughts, or gathered his head; his physical head was literally saved in those moments. King Herod had threatened Peter with beheading, thus silencing the spread of God's Word, but now after the miraculous rescue by the angel, Peter can think clearly. He says he is absolutely sure the Lord has delivered him. Prayer will be effective as it will invoke God's presence and action. Peter realizes he had not been dreaming; it had to be the activity of God that set him free.

Once Peter regains full consciousness, he quickly finds his way to the church. There the believers prayed for Peter, not knowing how God would answer, but knowing for "surety," truth above all, that He would answer. Although Peter was very much a believer and no doubt prayed for his own escape, the church needed to see for themselves how God heard them. Peter could not introduce the church to the angel, nor invite it in to explain how a blow to the side could both awaken him and removed his chains. All he had was his physical body as proof not only that he had escaped, but that God indeed answers prayer.

11 And when Peter was come to himself, he said, Now I know of a surety, that the Lord hath sent his angel, and hath delivered me out of the hand of Herod, and from all the expectation of the people of the Jews.

The withdrawal of the angel of the Lord corresponds to Peter's "coming to himself." The Greek phrase (en heauto ginomai; en he-ow-TOE GHEE-no-my) indicates that Peter's state of being changed. He was no longer sleeping but in waking consciousness. In this state, he is able to understand what has happened to him and that it was not simply a dream.

The phrase "now I know of a surety, that the Lord hath sent his angel" is a declaration that Peter is aware this whole ordeal was not a dream, but orchestrated by God. The word "surety" (Gk. *alethos*, **ah-ley-THOS**) means simply truth or reality. As in **Acts 12:3**, Luke joins the power of Herod to the hostile expectation of the Jews. Here the adverbial use of the term "expectation" (Gk. *prosdokia*, **pros-doe-KEE-ah**) is used. In the New Testament it is only used here and in **Luke 21:26**. The word can be used for positive or negative expectation. It is in the negative sense here, as Peter realizes that he has been rescued from the persecution of Herod and the vocal Jewish leadership who influenced him.

## SEARCH THE SCRIPTURES

### QUESTION 2
What three commands did the angel give Peter (vv. 7–8)?

### QUESTION 3
Peter thought that he was _____ ____ _____.

## BIBLE APPLICATION

AIM: You will learn that believers should pray together and expect God to answer.

The church is depicted in this lesson as a place of refuge and mutual support. Unfortunately, today the church seems to be the last place considered for those needs. It is very important that believers remember how unity is a common thread which God uses not only to build His kingdom, but also protect and love His people. Is the church today anything like the church that prayed for Paul?

## STUDENT'S RESPONSES

**AIM: You will learn that God can rescue people from dangerous circumstances.**

Often we pray without considering whether our prayers are heard. Instead of praying as an empty ritual, we can practice praying in faith that God will answer. Encourage the class to discuss and select an issue or current event for which they will pray over a period of time. Select someone in the class to monitor the situation and give a report of their prayers at work.

## PRAYER

Our Provider and our Deliverer, we are so grateful that You take care of us and provide a way out of no way. We worship and adore You for showing us Your mercy each and every day. In the Name of Jesus we pray. Amen.

## HOW TO SAY IT

Quaternions.     kwa-ter-**NEE**-yins.

Surety.          **SHER**-eh-tee.

## PREPARE FOR NEXT SUNDAY

Read **Acts 15:1–12** and "God Makes No Distinction."

### DAILY HOME BIBLE READINGS

**MONDAY**
The Rock That Saves
(Psalm 18:1–9)

**TUESDAY**
The Shepherd Who Restores
(Psalm 80:1–3, 7, 17–19)

**WEDNESDAY**
God Saves Daniel
(Daniel 6:19–23)

**THURSDAY**
The Faithful God
(Daniel 6:25–28)

**FRIDAY**
God Saves Paul
(Acts 27:14–25)

**SATURDAY**
The Freeing God
(Acts 12:12–18)

**SUNDAY**
God Rescues Peter
(Acts 12:1–11)

**Sources:**
Carson, D.A., France, R.T., Motyer, J.A., Wenham, J.G. *New Bible Commentary*. Downers Grove, IL: InterVarsity Press, 1993.
Keener, Craig S. *IVP Bible Background Commentary*. Downers Grove, IL: InterVarsity Press, 1993.
Polhill, John B. Acts. *New American Commentary: An Exegetical and Theological Exposition of Holy Scripture*. Nashville: B&H Publishing, 1992.

## COMMENTS / NOTES:

_____
_____
_____
_____
_____
_____
_____
_____
_____
_____
_____
_____
_____
_____
_____
_____
_____
_____
_____

# GOD MAKES NO DISTINCTION

**BIBLE BASIS:** ACTS 15:1–12

**BIBLE TRUTH:** Luke claimed that the Jerusalem council had power to change the Law of Moses in order to make it congruent to God's action.

**MEMORY VERSES:** "And God, which knoweth the hearts, bare them witness, giving them the Holy Ghost, even as he did unto us; And put no difference between us and them, purifying their hearts by faith" (Acts 15:8–9).

**LESSON AIM:** By the end of this lesson, we will: REVIEW the story of how the Jerusalem council listened to Paul and Barnabas as they told of the signs and wonders God did among the Gentiles; REFLECT on how difficult it can be to reconcile law and God's action; and INITIATE a process of discernment of God's will when the law and God's actions appear to conflict.

## LESSON SCRIPTURE

### ACTS 15:1–12, KJV

1 And certain men which came down from Judaea taught the brethren, and said, Except ye be circumcised after the manner of Moses, ye cannot be saved.

2 When therefore Paul and Barnabas had no small dissension and disputation with them, they determined that Paul and Barnabas, and certain other of them, should go up to Jerusalem unto the apostles and elders about this question.

3 And being brought on their way by the church, they passed through Phenice and Samaria, declaring the conversion of the Gentiles: and they caused great joy unto all the brethren.

4 And when they were come to Jerusalem, they were received of the church, and of the apostles and elders, and they declared all things that God had done with them.

5 But there rose up certain of the sect of the Pharisees which believed, saying, That it was needful to circumcise them, and to command them to keep the law of Moses.

6 And the apostles and elders came together for to consider of this matter.

7 And when there had been much disputing, Peter rose up, and said unto them, Men and brethren, ye know how that a good while ago God made choice among us, that the Gentiles by my mouth should hear the word of the gospel, and believe.

8 And God, which knoweth the hearts, bare them witness, giving them the Holy Ghost, even as he did unto us;

9 And put no difference between us and them, purifying their hearts by faith.

10 Now therefore why tempt ye God, to put a yoke upon the neck of the disciples, which neither our fathers nor we were able to bear?

11 But we believe that through the grace of the Lord Jesus Christ we shall be saved, even as they.

12 Then all the multitude kept silence, and gave audience to Barnabas and Paul, declaring what miracles and wonders God had

wrought among the Gentiles by them.

## LIFE NEED FOR TODAY'S LESSON

**AIM: You will see how laws are an integral part of civilized society, and that some laws must change as society changes. However, no law will negate or supersede God.**

## INTRODUCTION

### The Radical Movement

The events recorded in the book of Acts reflect a period marked by political and social upheaval. While the ancient world was no stranger to religious debates, the absolutely radical movement incited by Jesus and His disciples was continuing to make waves. As the early church was developing, it was still very much a sect of Judaism, since Jesus and His disciples were committed to their Hebrew roots. Nevertheless, just as Jesus had to stand against the rulers, high priests, and Pharisees, so now would His disciples, both original and newly converted, have to contend with those who attempted to straddle the line between grace and the law. The central debate in this passage centers on the Jews' historical separation from Gentiles. The conversion of Cornelius and his household in **Acts 10–11** sparked a controversy that epitomized the explosive birth and growth of the Christian church.

## BIBLE LEARNING

**AIM: You will discover that Paul and Barnabas shared the power of God's mighty acts in the Gentile community.**

## I. GOD'S WILL DEBATED (Acts 15:1–3)

The "certain men" who initiated the circumcision controversy in the early church are known as Judaizers. Their desire to navigate the demands of God's Law and His grace

would not be the first or last such attempt in the life of the church. While it is difficult to imagine a modern debate of this type, it is not unlike the various divisions that have created the many different denominations of the Christian faith. It is true that circumcision was indeed God's command, initially given to Abraham in **Genesis 17:10**.

Notably, Paul and Barnabas were chosen to discuss the case against physical circumcision on their journey. Paul, especially, was no stranger to Jewish tradition and law, at times recalling the depth of his religious pedigree (**Philippians 3:4–6**). Additionally, Paul had the unique position of being both the chief persecutor of the church (**Acts 9:1–5**) as well as one of its most prolific champions. In preparation for the debate ahead, it is important to note that they stopped to report the effect of the Gospel message on the Gentiles along the way. Their emphasis on the salvation of Gentiles is important as it helped to verify the authenticity of the Gospel's power among those not born Jews. Of course the result of their report is the "great joy" experienced by the brethren. The Christian message is ultimately joy that comes individually to those who accept eternal life, and collectively as more are added to the Body of Christ.

## Acts 15:1–12

15:1 And certain men which came down from Judaea taught the brethren, and said, Except ye be circumcised after the manner of Moses, ye cannot be saved. 2 When therefore Paul and Barnabas had no small dissension and disputation with them, they determined that Paul and Barnabas, and certain other of them, should go up to Jerusalem unto the apostles and elders about this question. 3 And being brought on their way by the church, they passed through Phenice and Samaria, declaring the conversion of the

**Gentiles: and they caused great joy unto all the brethren.**

Some say these "certain men" were (1) proselytes to the Jewish religion, (2) the Pharisees, or (3) priests who were obedient to the Jewish faith. Whoever they were, they were recent Jewish converts to Christianity. The men arrived in Antioch from Judea. They came to Antioch, the headquarters of those who preached to the Gentiles, preaching a doctrine different from what Paul, Barnabas, and the other leaders of Christianity taught. Their message to the Gentile Christians was that they would now have to submit to circumcision and the Jewish ceremonial law. They taught that unless people were circumcised after the manner (Gk. *ethos*, **EE-thoce**) or customs prescribed by the law, they were not saved. Although many of the Jews embraced Christianity, they did not want to release their Jewish heritage and customs. Not only did they continue to observe Jewish rituals and laws, some also wanted to impose these requirements on the Gentile Christians.

Many Jews at this time believed that Gentiles would be saved by keeping the seven Noahide laws (**Genesis 9:1–7**). These were the laws the Jews believed were binding for all people because they were given to Noah, the ancestor of all the people to repopulate the earth after the Flood. Other Jews believed Gentiles could only be right with God by observing the whole Torah, including the ceremonial laws. For men this meant circumcision, and for both genders it meant observance of dietary laws. This debate about what was required for Gentiles spilled over into the open argument in **Acts 15**.

Paul, Barnabas, and the other leaders of the Gentile Christians would not see the truth betrayed or distorted. They taught: (1) Christ came to free us from the yoke of ceremonial law, (2) Jews and Gentiles were united in Christ, and (3) salvation comes by belief in Jesus Christ. Baptism and the Lord's Supper were the two ritual instructions given to the church. Paul and the other leaders could not bear to hear of circumcising the Gentile converts because God had already affirmed the acceptance of Gentiles by filling them with the Holy Spirit. Those Judaizers who came with this doctrine claimed they came at the directions of the apostles and elders at Jerusalem. Therefore, the church at Antioch appointed Paul and Barnabas to go to Jerusalem to present this case to the apostles and elders. Since the apostles and elders established Christianity in Jerusalem, their opinion in this matter was very crucial. It was necessary to hear what they had to say in order to put an end to the controversy, and to silence these teachers and false apostles.

Paul and Barnabas traveled or passed through Phenice or Phoenicia and Samaria declaring (*ekdiegeomai*, **ek-dee-ay-GEH-oh-my**) which means to narrate in full or wholly the conversion of the Gentiles. The word for conversion (*epistrophe*, **eh-pee-stroh-FAY**) means a turning about or turning around. Their report resulted in joy for all the church.

## II. GOD'S WILL CONSIDERED (vv. 4–6)

Some would discourage debate among believers, seeing it as a sign of division. Yet, God encourages His children to seek His will actively and engage each other with Scripture, prayer, and a desire for unity. This quest for unity seems to be the missing element to the discussion initiated by the Judaizers. As a result, Paul and Barnabas must engage in what amounts to a trial to plead the case for grace against the position of the law, which mandated circumcision. This trial pointed toward the definition of what true belief would come to mean.

Today's debates rarely involve physical alteration of the body; however, many religious rites and activities must be carefully considered not only for their historical significance, but also their spiritual relevance. The apostles and elders coming together to discuss a difficult situation presents a great role model for the contemporary church to follow. While there were legitimate foundations to both sides of the debate, it was certainly worth discussing, rather than initiating war, or worse, dismantling the newborn church for lack of an agreement. Many issues face new and modern believers, which should be discussed with careful consideration of God's will, versus the desires of psychological comfort or blind tradition.

**4 And when they were come to Jerusalem, they were received of the church, and of the apostles and elders, and they declared all things that God had done with them. 5 But there rose up certain of the sect of the Pharisees which believed, saying, That it was needful to circumcise them, and to command them to keep the law of Moses. 6 And the apostles and elders came together for to consider of this matter.**

Finally Paul and Barnabas arrive in Jerusalem and Luke notes that they were received (*apo-dechomai*, **ah-po-DEH-kho-my**) or heartily welcomed by the church and the apostles and elders. They also declare all the things that God had done. The focus is on what God is doing among the Gentiles as this is Paul and Barnabas' unique ministry task.

As much as they are received by the church they also face opposition. This opposition arises from a sect (*hairesis*, **HIGH-ray-sees**) which means a group of people following their own tenets. In this context it refers to a certain group of Pharisees who are given to the same beliefs and practices within the wider group of Pharisees. These men claimed the Gentiles' conversion

was not complete. In their opinion, the Gentile Christians needed to be circumcised and to keep the law of Moses.

At the Jerusalem council, the apostles and elders gathered by consent to consider this matter. They came to reason together. They did not give their judgment separately or rashly, but considered the matter rationally and communally. The apostles, although of higher authority than the elders, did not exclude them. Here is an example to the leaders of churches, pastors in particular, when disputes arise (and they will): come together in solemn meeting for mutual advice and encouragement. Bring all together to present their positions so that the church can act in concert and come to the best decision for all involved.

## SEARCH THE SCRIPTURES

### QUESTION 1
What topic did Paul and Barnabas need to address for new converts?

### QUESTION 2
State the two cities that both Paul and Barnabas traveled to share the Gospel.

## III. GOD'S WILL REVEALED (vv. 7–12)

As Peter adds his voice to the fervent debate, his words bring a severe but comforting resolution. He uses several words that ring out even in sermons to this day. "God made [a] choice…" While Peter is specifically speaking about his inspiration to proclaim the Gospel to the Gentiles, he is echoing the foundation of both the Jewish and now Christian faith. God's choice was to save His people. This was announced by prophets and by various acts of God all through Scripture. If God has initially chosen who would speak, He has now chosen who may hear and subsequently believe. This is a radical concept considering the Judaizers' lifelong understanding of being "God's chosen" as an elite group, free to discriminate and exclude outsiders.

A chilling summary follows as he declares that God put "no difference between us and them" (v. 9) and acknowledges that the rigors of the law were even too much for the Jewish ancestors to bear. Even those who are fully committed to the law are incapable of obeying it completely without fail. To acknowledge this simple human frailty is the first step to embracing the call of God and the power of the Holy Spirit.

Peter's conclusion should motivate anyone attempting to engage in evangelism. The difference between "we" and "they" should never last long in a believer's view of another person. It is simply a matter of timing. Jesus' commission to go, teach, and baptize (Matthew 28:19–20, Mark 16:15–16) means that everyone can have an opportunity not only to be called brother and sister, but also be acknowledged as the sons and daughters of God.

7 And when there had been much disputing, Peter rose up, and said unto them, Men and brethren, ye know that a good while ago God made choice among us, that the Gentiles by my mouth should hear the word of the Gospel, and believe. 8 And God, which knoweth the hearts, bare them witness, giving them the Holy Ghost, even as he did unto us; 9 And put no difference between us and them, purifying their hearts by faith. 10 Now therefore why tempt ye God, to put a yoke upon the neck of the disciples, which neither our fathers nor we were able to bear? 11 But we believe that through the grace of the Lord Jesus Christ we shall be saved, even as they. 12 Then all the multitude kept silence and gave audience to Barnabas and Paul, declaring what miracles and wonders God had wrought among the Gentiles by them.

After much disputing (Gk. *suzetesis*, su-ZAY-tay-sees) or mutual questioning and discussion on both sides, the Apostle Peter stood to address the group. Peter was the first apostle to preach to a Gentile audience (Acts 10:34–43). He reminded them of his experience in preaching the Gospel to the Gentiles. When Peter reported his experience to the Jerusalem church, everyone rejoiced and no one said a word about circumcision (Acts 11:1–18).

Peter uses the compound word *kardiognostes* (Gk. kar-dee-ah-NOS-tays). This word is used in the Bible only in the book of Acts. In both instances it (there are only two) is in reference to God and His omniscience (1:24; 15:8). This is in anticipation of Peter confirming that God gave them the Holy Spirit. He says that God "bare them witness" (Gk. *martureo*, mar-too-REH-oh). Peter is letting the council know that God knows people's hearts and therefore knows what He is doing.

Peter went on to say that since God did not differentiate between the Gentiles and the Jews, His followers should not either. The Gentiles were as welcome to the grace of Jesus Christ as the Jews. Their hearts were purified (Gk. *katharizo*, ka-tha-REED-zo) by faith. The word for purified is the same word for pronouncing something clean in the Levitical sense. It is used in Acts 10:15 as God speaks to Peter about clean and unclean food. Now this word is used for the Gentiles. They are no longer "unclean" people because their hearts have been cleansed through faith in Christ. Paul reiterated this point to the church at Galatia: God would not deny anyone who believes in Jesus Christ access to the Holy Spirit. There is no distinction between Christians in Christ (Galatians 3:28).

Peter reproved those who wanted to bring the Gentiles under the obligation of the law of Moses. In his indictment against the Jewish leaders, he basically asks why they would want to test God when they can see how powerfully

He is moving. In this case, to tempt (Gk. *peirazo*, **pay-ROD-zo**) means to exhibit distrust (**Matthew 16:1**) and it is Peter's way of saying not to go against the movement God has already started to bring the Gentiles to faith. In other words, trust what the Holy Spirit is doing. The Jewish ceremonial law was a heavy yoke (Gk. *zugos*, **zoo-GOHS**) that no one could keep. The yoke was a device that joined two cattle together as they plowed in the field; hence it became used metaphorically for any type of burden or bondage. A yoke could also have a positive connotation of strong support and guidance as in **Lamentations 3:27** or with the yoke of rabbinic instruction. Jesus Christ came to set us free from the yoke of the law, saying, "Take my yoke upon you and learn of me, for I am gentle and humble in heart, and you will find rest for your souls" (**Matthew 11:29, NIV**).

Peter reminds the Jerusalem church leaders that the salvation they received comes by the grace (Gk. *charis*, **KHAH-rees**) or unmerited favor of Jesus Christ. It is not by circumcision or uncircumcision, but by grace through faith in Jesus Christ. They could not obtain salvation by keeping the law. Peter confessed that neither they nor their ancestors could bear up under this weight. Both Jews and Gentiles are now equal in God's eyes and will receive the same salvation because of Christ.

"All the multitude" refers to the believers who were present for the council. These believers kept silent in order to give audience to (Gk. *akouo*, **ah-KOO-oh**) or hear what Paul and Barnabas said. Their accounts are found in **Acts 13 and 14.** During these occasions, their preaching of the Gospel included not only readings from the Law and Prophets and the retelling of God's salvation of Israel, but also signs and wonders were wrought (Gk. *poieo*, **poy-EH-oh**) or worked among the Gentiles. This showed the approval of God on this new work of preaching the Gospel to the Gentiles.

To impose the whole Law of Moses now would subvert what God had already begun.

## SEARCH THE SCRIPTURES
### QUESTION 3
What does multitude refer to in **verse 12**? Share the response of the "multitude" to Peter and Barnabas.

## BIBLE APPLICATION

**AIM: You will understand why Christians should remember that it is important to know that God gives everyone an equal opportunity.**

Many people would not know the first thing about another method of worship outside their own. Even among Christian denominations, there seem to be sharp divisions between the practices of the Baptists, Presbyterians, Episcopalians, Pentecostals, Methodists, Catholics, etc. While there are many styles and even many administrations of worship that are ordained by Scripture (**1 Corinthians 12:5**), there is still only one Lord, one faith, and one baptism (**Ephesians 4:5**). It is the confession of Jesus Christ and faith in Him that unites us all.

## STUDENT'S RESPONSES

**AIM: You will learn that Christians understand that it can be difficult to choose between God's laws and society's laws.**

God desires unity among all believers in Christ so that we may operate as one body (**1 Corinthians 12:12**). However, the reality is that this desire is often thwarted by believers on numerous levels. One of the ways we can seek out unity is learning how to resolve conflict in a Christlike manner. As a class, construct a model for conflict resolution based on the events in **Acts 15**. Note the different elements that helped the early church to come to a peaceful resolution regarding the circumcision of Gentile believers.

## PRAYER

Thank You, Jesus, for choosing us and giving everyone an opportunity to know You. Like Paul and Barnabas, we want to stand firm on Your word as we speak to others about who You are. In the Name of Jesus, we pray. Amen.

## HOW TO SAY IT

Disputation     dis-pyu-**TAY**-shun.

Phenice     fe-**NEES**.

## PREPARE FOR NEXT SUNDAY

Read **Acts 16:1–5, 8–15** and "From Derbe to Philippi."

### DAILY HOME BIBLE READINGS

**MONDAY**
Thanking God
(Romans 1:8–15)

**TUESDAY**
The Forgiving God
(Nehemiah 9:6–21)

**WEDNESDAY**
Abundant Grace
(Romans 16:25–27)

**THURSDAY**
Accessible God
(Hebrews 4:12–16)

**FRIDAY**
God is Making All Things New
(Revelation 21:1–5)

**SATURDAY**
Grace for Gentiles
(Galatians 3:6–14)

**SUNDAY**
God Makes No Distinction
(Acts 15:1–12)

**Sources:**

Carson, D.A., France, R.T., Motyer, J.A., Wenham, J.G. *New Bible Commentary*. Downers Grove, IL: InterVarsity Press, 1993.

Keener, Craig S. *IVP Bible Background Commentary*. Downers Grove, IL: InterVarsity Press, 1993.

Polhill, John B. *Acts. New American Commentary: An Exegetical and Theological Exposition of Holy Scripture*. Nashville: B&H Publishing, 1992.

## COMMENTS / NOTES:

_____
_____
_____
_____
_____
_____
_____
_____
_____
_____
_____
_____
_____
_____
_____
_____
_____
_____
_____
_____
_____
_____
_____
_____
_____
_____

# FROM DERBE TO PHILIPPI

**BIBLE BASIS:** ACTS 16:1–5, 8–15

**BIBLE TRUTH:** Paul's obedience to God and his respect for the elders and apostles gave opportunities for the Gospel to spread to many regions.

**MEMORY VERSE:** "And after he had seen the vision, immediately we endeavoured to go into Macedonia, assuredly gathering that the Lord had called us for to preach the gospel unto them" (Acts 16:10).

**LESSON AIM:** By the end of the lesson, we will: RECALL how Paul added Timothy to his missionary team and their labors in spreading the Gospel from Derbe to Philippi; REFLECT on those characteristics needed for members of a successful evangelism team; and SPREAD the Gospel in every aspect of our lives.

## LESSON SCRIPTURE

### ACTS 16:1–5, 8–15, KJV

1 Then came he to Derbe and Lystra: and, behold, a certain disciple was there, named Timotheus, the son of a certain woman, which was a Jewess, and believed; but his father was a Greek:

2 Which was well reported of by the brethren that were at Lystra and Iconium.

3 Him would Paul have to go forth with him; and took and circumcised him because of the Jews which were in those quarters: for they knew all that his father was a Greek.

4 And as they went through the cities, they delivered them the decrees for to keep, that were ordained of the apostles and elders which were at Jerusalem.

5 And so were the churches established in the faith, and increased in number daily.

8 And they passing by Mysia came down to Troas.

9 And a vision appeared to Paul in the night; There stood a man of Macedonia, and prayed him, saying, Come over into Macedonia, and help us.

10 And after he had seen the vision, immediately we endeavoured to go into Macedonia, assuredly gathering that the Lord had called us for to preach the gospel unto them.

11 Therefore loosing from Troas, we came with a straight course to Samothracia, and the next day to Neapolis;

12 And from thence to Philippi, which is the chief city of that part of Macedonia, and a colony: and we were in that city abiding certain days.

13 And on the sabbath we went out of the city by a river side, where prayer was wont to be made; and we sat down, and spake unto the women which resorted thither.

14 And a certain woman named Lydia, a seller of purple, of the city of Thyatira, which worshipped God, heard us: whose heart the Lord opened, that she attended unto the things which were spoken of Paul.

15 And when she was baptized, and her household, she besought us, saying, If ye have judged me to be faithful to the Lord, come into my house, and abide there. And she constrained us.

## LIFE NEED FOR TODAY'S LESSON

AIM: **You will learn that sometimes things that start out small, turn out much larger than expected, and impact the lives of others in surprising ways.**

## INTRODUCTION

### Differing Cultures

After Paul's first missionary journey (**Acts 13–14**), a debate began raging in the churches at Antioch, Cilicia, and Syria regarding the nature of Christian salvation and how new Gentile believers were to fit into the new Christian church. Regarding salvation, some argued that faith in Christ wasn't enough to be saved, but Jewish Christians must also strictly follow Mosaic Law in order to consider themselves saved (**Acts 15:1**). Additionally, they insisted that Gentile believers must also be circumcised in keeping with the law of Moses.

A meeting was held in Jerusalem to resolve the issue. The Jerusalem council (**Acts 15:1–35**) determined that both Jewish and Gentile believers are saved by grace through faith in Christ alone. Gentile believers were not expected to adhere to Jewish customs. However, they outlined a few directives that would help Gentiles avoid offending fellow Jewish believers. For example, Gentiles didn't have to follow the same dietary laws as Jews, but were directed to abstain from eating "meats offered to idols, and from blood, and from things strangled" (**v. 29, KJV**).

## BIBLE LEARNING

AIM: **You will learn that Lydia listened to Paul's preaching and then was baptized along with her other family members.**

## I. PAUL RECRUITS TIMOTHY (Acts 16:1–5)

When Paul and Silas met Timothy at Lystra, Timothy had already garnered a good reputation among the believers in Lystra and Iconium. This ecclesial witness of Timothy's suitability as a teacher was why Paul chose him to join them. His father was Greek and his mother was Jewish. It was Greek tradition for a child to follow after his father's religion. However, Jewish tradition held that a child was considered Jewish if his mother was Jewish. Paul knew that in the eyes of the Jewish people they would be ministering to, Timothy would be seen as a Jew and would therefore need to be circumcised to avoid offense. This was not in contradiction with the church's earlier ruling that Gentile converts need not be circumcised for salvation (**Acts 15:10–11, 19**).

Paul's ministry journeys were meant to help establish and maintain new churches as well as communicate the decisions and positions made by the leaders in Jerusalem. This was an important part of cultivating the unity of the early church. The believers' faith and confidence in the Gospel was increased.

## Acts 16:1–5, 8–15

16:1 Then came he to Derbe and Lystra: and, behold, a certain disciple was there, named Timotheus, the son of a certain woman, which was a Jewess, and believed; but his father was a Greek: 2 Which was well reported of by the brethren that were at Lystra and Iconium. 3 Him would Paul have to go forth with him; and took and circumcised him because of the Jews which were in those quarters: for they knew all that his father was a Greek. 4 And as they went through the cities, they delivered them the decrees for to keep, that were ordained of the apostles and elders which were at Jerusalem.

**5 And so were the churches established in the faith, and increased in number daily.**

On their second missionary journey, Paul and Silas traveled north around the eastern end of the Mediterranean and then westward toward the cities of Derbe and Lystra. On this second journey, the order of the cities listed in the Galatian territory is reversed from the first journey. On their first visit to the Galatian territory, Paul and Barnabas traveled from the west rather than the east. On this second journey, Paul revisits the cities that had been evangelized during his first journey two or three years earlier. When Paul and Barnabas began their ministry in Lystra, the people believed they were Greek gods (**14:11–13**). Their short ministry in the Galatian cities ended with Paul's being stoned and left for dead outside the walls of Lystra. However, one of the fruits of that short, violent time was a young man named Timothy. Timothy and his mother may have been among the group of disciples that surrounded the apparently lifeless body of the apostle outside the walls of Lystra after Jews from the cities of Iconium and Antioch had stoned Paul (**vv. 19–20**). The young man certainly would have been among those Paul confirmed on his second visit to the city, exhorting them "to continue in the faith" (**v. 22**).

Timothy's mother was a Jewess (Gk. *ioudaias*, **eu-DIE-ahs**), which is the feminine form of the word for Jew, and also a Christian. The fact that she had married a Greek and had not circumcised her son leads one to question whether she was a practicing Jew before her conversion. Such mixed marriages, though practiced little and disliked by the stricter Jews in Palestine, probably occurred frequently among the Jews of the dispersion, and in such instances if the father was Greek, sons were unlikely to be circumcised because Judaism was still passed down through the father during the first century AD. Even at a young age, Timothy was well reported of by the brethren who were at Lystra and Iconium. The phrase "well reported of" (Gk. *martureo*, **mar-too-REH-oh**) comes from the Greek word for "witness," which in the passive voice means to be witnessed about and is usually used in a positive context.

During the years Paul was away, Timothy had grown in faith, so Paul decided to take the young man under his wing. He asked Timothy to join him and Silas on their journey. Timothy was the first Gentile who became a missionary after his conversion. Later, Titus would join Paul, but he would not be circumcised because he was a true Gentile (**Galatians 2:3**). Mosaic Law commanded that at eight days old, all Hebrew boys were to undergo the rite of circumcision. After God reconfirmed His promise to Abraham for the third and last time, He said of Abraham's descendants, "Any uncircumcised male, who has not been circumcised in the flesh, will be cut off from his people; he has broken my covenant" (**Genesis 17:14**). This meant the uncircumcised Israelite male was not covered by the covenant promise given to Abraham. The rite of circumcision symbolized submission to God and faith in His promise.

Circumcision was not carried over into the church as a requirement for Gentiles. Still, many Jewish Christians tried to impose circumcision and the Mosaic Law on new Gentile believers (**Acts 15:1**). But the Jerusalem council rejected the requirement (**15:1–29**). In mixed marriages, Jewish mothers were not permitted to circumcise their sons against the Gentile father's wishes. Paul had Timothy circumcised because of his parentage. Paul's methodology was to preach the Gospel to the Jew first, then the Gentile. But such a course would have been impossible had Timothy as a Jew not been circumcised; his own people would have rejected him and dismissed the Gospel message.

The new threesome continued their ministry in Derbe, Lystra, Iconium, other cities in Lycaonia, and in Phrygia and Galatia. They advised the churches in these cities and taught rules of Christian conduct, such as those concerning the Gentiles' abstinence from blood, things strangled, fornication, and from things offered to idols (**Acts 15:20–29**). As a result of these apostolic visits, the churches were established (Gk. *stereoo*, **steh-reh-OH-oh**) or strengthened and the number of believers increased (Gk. *perisseuo*, **peh-rees-SOO-oh**) or multiplied daily. The word for "increased" or "abound" is also the word for a flower coming to full bloom. Luke makes it clear that the Jerusalem council's decree was for the church's well-being.

## II. A DIVINE CHANGE OF PLANS (vv. 8–12)

Troas was an important Greek port, located near ancient Troy, that sat between the landmasses of Europe and Asia Minor. During their time at Troas, Paul has a vision of a man from Macedonia calling out to him for help. Paul and his group immediately take this vision to mean that they must alter their course and travel to Macedonia. This act of obedience to God's will is historically pivotal in that it eventually results in the Gospel being spread further west into Europe. If Paul and his group had not been sensitive to how God was trying to lead them, they might have missed this important change in their plans. This also underlines why it was important that they chose their ministry partners carefully. These decisions regarding how God was leading them forward were ultimately made as a group.

It is important to note that in **verse 10**, the language changes to "we" rather than "they," which is used earlier in the chapter. This indicates that Luke, the author of Acts, was actually present during this leg of Paul's ministry travels.

8 And they passing by Mysia came down to Troas. 9 And a vision appeared to Paul in the night; There stood a man of Macedonia, and prayed him, saying, Come over into Macedonia, and help us. 10 And after he had seen the vision, immediately we endeavoured to go into Macedonia, assuredly gathering that the Lord had called us for to preach the gospel unto them. 11 Therefore loosing from Troas, we came with a straight course to Samothracia, and the next day to Neapolis; 12 And from thence to Philippi, which is the chief city of that part of Macedonia, and a colony: and we were in that city abiding certain days.

Still traveling over rugged terrain and past unevangelized regions, the apostles passed by another city devoid of ministry and hospitality on the way to their appointed destination. God, through the Holy Spirit, was their travel agent, and the apostles relied solely on God's timing to fulfill His will. Arriving at Mysia, they attempted to enter, but the Holy Ghost prevented them from doing so. Now twice denied access to a people in need of the Gospel message, the apostles no doubt questioned whether they were going in the right direction. Even while waiting for God to open doors, these disciples did not assume a passive posture.

Instead, they participated with active pursuit of God's will—ever going until He said "Stop!" A wide door stood open for them when they came to Troas. The city of Troas was located near the Hellespont, an economically vibrant intersection of race, class, culture, and language. Imagine the cacophony of sounds, smells, philosophies, theologies, dress, and demeanor on display at Troas. It was in this place of diversity that the Holy Spirit released the disciples to minister.

The Greek noun *horama* (**HO-rah-mah**), or "vision," is a sight divinely granted, sometimes while sleeping (**Acts 9:10, 12, 18:9**). It is likely that Paul was asleep when this vision appeared, yet he was fully aware of God's purpose and presence in this vision. The Holy Ghost forbade (**v. 6**) and prevented (**v. 7**) the disciples' movement previously; here the Spirit manifests Himself in a form and function believable to them. The Greek verb *parakaleo* (**pa-ra-ka-LEH-oh**), or "prayed," connotes the image of one begging for consolation, instruction, or teaching. This man from Macedonia showed up in Paul's dream pleading with passion and urgency for the apostles to come to this Roman province to help with some urgent cause that had not been met by all of Rome's prestige, privilege, or military prowess.

After Paul communicated the vision to his companions, they immediately responded to this Word from the Lord. Here, companionship in ministry is illuminated as Luke records this first-person plural account that "we endeavoured" (Gk. *zeteo*, **dzay-TEH-oh**), or made a concerted effort, to get to Macedonia. Included in this group were at least Paul, Silas, Timothy, and Luke. This inclusive reference establishes a paradigm of Christian companionship and community that becomes a predominant theme in the rest of Paul's letters to the church. This time, unlike the holy hindrances in **verses 6 and 7**, their collaborative effort to carry the Gospel to the next place of ministry was allowed. Note also that consensus was taken to test whether this vision was from the Lord. Although God spoke through visions, not every vision was unquestionably believed. Upon determining that this was the Holy Spirit's leading ("assuredly gathering"), the apostles acted together with urgency to respond to the vision.

As the disciples were loosing (Gk. *anago*, **ah-NAH-go**) or launching on a boat out from Troas, even the wind was in their favor, providing a straight, smooth course in two days through two ports to their stated destination—Philippi. This Macedonian city was a Roman colony. The inhabitants of such colonies were protected and privileged as full-fledged Roman citizens. Some of the privileges of being a Roman colony were voting rights, preferential legislation, and immunity from taxation.

## SEARCH THE SCRIPTURES

### QUESTION 1
Timotheus was the son of a Jewish and _____ mother and his father was _____ (**v. 1**).

## III. LYDIA'S HEART IS OPENED (vv. 13–15)

According to Jewish law, ten males were needed for public worship. If there was no established synagogue, worshipers were to gather in an open area, near a body of water. Apparently, Philippi had no synagogue, since Paul and his men went to a nearby riverbank to find people who would be praying. The nearest body of water was likely a tributary to the Gangites (modern Angitis), which was 1.25 miles from Philippi.

As Paul and his men talked to a gathering of women, they caught the ear of Lydia, a merchant from Thyatira. Thyatira was known for its merchants of dyed cloth, particularly purple material. It has been suggested that purple dyes were created from shellfish or the roots of plants. Lydia "worshipped God" (**v. 14**), which indicates that she was a Gentile who worshiped Yahweh, but was not saved and not part of the Christian church.

13 And on the sabbath we went out of the city by a river side, where prayer was wont to be made; and we sat down, and spake unto the

women which resorted thither. 14 And a certain woman named Lydia, a seller of purple, of the city of Thyatira, which worshipped God, heard us: whose heart the Lord opened, that she attended unto the things which were spoken of Paul. 15 And when she was baptized, and her household, she besought us, saying, If ye have judged me to be faithful to the Lord, come into my house, and abide there. And she constrained us.

"Sabbath" (Gk. *sabbaton*, **SAB-ba-ton**) is the seventh day of each week, a sacred day when the Israelites were required to abstain from all work. On the Sabbath, it was customary to gather for worship, prayer, and Scripture reading. Although the apostles could have taken a day off from the work of preaching the Gospel, they were compelled to leave the accommodations in Philippi and journey a mile or two west of the city to a prayer meeting down by the Gangites River. Here, the disciples find women praying to God in a place outside the city where there was no synagogue. No doubt following the leading of the Holy Spirit, the apostles did not bypass or dismiss this gathering of women worshiping God on the Sabbath. Modeling Jesus' radical paradigm of teaching to the outcasts, the disciples were not constrained by gender (**Galatians 3:28**) nor limited by their surroundings when teaching and preaching God's Word. All they required was that hearts were open to hear what the Spirit was saying to the church.

For a synagogue to be established in a city, ten Jewish men had to convene and lead it. With no synagogue in Philippi at this time, the apostles sought out a prayer gathering whose reputation trumped Jewish ritual. This prayer meeting had the structure and leadership of a worship service, including the reading of Jewish prayers and praying to the God of Abraham, Isaac, and Jacob. In the absence of ten male heads of household to found a

synagogue, the women were found faithfully worshiping God in spirit and in truth (**John 4:23–24**). Through the apostles, the Holy Spirit of God brought forth the first evangelistic converts in Europe. He did this in this holy place, set up and sanctified by women. It is while attending to the divine act of worship that a certain woman and a gathering of women became the first European converts to our Christian faith. Women's work and women's worship should be heralded in biblical and local church history as integral, not incidental, to the Good News.

Lydia was a woman of Thyatira, the city of commerce, and a seller of purple cloth often used for official Roman garments. She was the first European convert of Paul and his hostess during his first stay at Philippi. Lydia was a businesswoman who was wealthy and well-respected, and who "worshipped" (Gk. *sebomai*, **SEH-bo-my**) God. The relationship she had with God was awe and reverential fear. While leading this prayer gathering, Lydia welcomed the opportunity to hear the apostles preach and teach, and to learn more about the God she worshiped and Christ, His Son. Lydia's enthusiastic and attentive listening was fertile ground for God to open her heart to understand and accept the Gospel. The "heart" (Gk. *kardia*, **kar-DEE-ah**) represents the soul or mind as the resident place of one's thoughts, passions, desires, appetites, affections, purposes, understanding, intelligence, will, character, and intentions. Lydia's "open heart surgery" was appreciably more than an emotional response to well-crafted rhetoric; as she listened, Lydia engaged her thoughts, affections, and understanding about God to believe in Christ Jesus. While Lydia had been seeking God, God was in the background working His way into her heart and into the city of Philippi.

Lydia's response to accepting the Gospel of Christ Jesus was to be baptized (Gk. *baptizo*, bap-TEED-zo), meaning to immerse or submerge in water. Since they were already gathered at the riverside, it was convenient to baptize Lydia and her household immediately following their conversion.

Lydia was not the only person present at the prayer meeting listening to Paul and his companions preach and teach. Her whole household (meaning both family members and servants) heard the Good News, believed, and were baptized. After becoming a baptized member of the church, Lydia extended hospitality to her newfound family—the apostles and by extension the church. She was so emphatic to extend hospitality to these brothers in Christ that she "constrained" (Gk. *parabiazomai*, **pa-ra-bee-AHD-zo-my**), or made a persuasive appeal, for them to stay at her home while in Philippi. Central to this plea for them to accept her hospitality was Lydia's assertion that the apostles found her "faithful" (Gk. *pistos*, **PIS-toce**), meaning trustworthy and reliable. This word also has the connotation of belonging to the faith community.

## SEARCH THE SCRIPTURES

### QUESTION 2
Lydia was from what city and a seller of what color cloth (v. 14)?

### QUESTION 3
Lydia was the first European convert to Christianity. True or False?

## BIBLE APPLICATION

**AIM: You will discover that believers should be sensitive to God's plan for their lives and open to change.**

Adaptability, agility, flexibility, versatility—these are all words commonly used to describe the ideal business in today's ever-changing global economy. The ability to change course quickly based on new information is a skill that companies are always trying to cultivate or acquire.

This same ability is important in our daily personal and spiritual lives. A healthy, growing relationship with Christ involves being able to adjust to what He is doing in and through us. When we yield ourselves to His plans and purposes, we can be sure that we're where God wants us.

## STUDENT'S RESPONSES

**AIM: Believers can participate in the expansion of the Kingdom of God as they actively and willingly do God's will.**

It can be hard to give up control of our plans for our lives. This can especially be hard after we've begun moving down a path that we believe God has led us down. Review your current goals and plans. Ask God to reveal any areas where you've allowed your personal ideas and ambitions to crowd out what God may be leading you to do instead.

## PRAYER

Bless You, O Lord, for providing us with so many opportunities to know You and to love You. Give us the wisdom to choose You God and to walk in Your faithfulness. In the Name of Jesus, we pray. Amen.

## HOW TO SAY IT

| | |
|---|---|
| Derbe. | der-BAY. |
| Lystra. | loo-STRAH. |
| Phrygia. | froo-GEE-ah. |

## PREPARE FOR NEXT SUNDAY

Read **Acts 17:1–4, 10–12, 22–25, 28** and "Thessalonica, Berea, and Athens."

---

### DAILY HOME BIBLE READINGS

**MONDAY**
The Way We Should Go
(Jeremiah 26:1–6)

**TUESDAY**
Boundless Riches of Christ
(Ephesians 3:7–12)

**WEDNESDAY**
Generosity of God
(Ezekiel 36:22–30)

**THURSDAY**
The Cost of Following
(Matthew 8:18–22)

**FRIDAY**
Paul and Silas in Prison
(Acts 16:16–24)

**SATURDAY**
Paul and Silas Escape
(Acts 16:25–40)

**SUNDAY**
From Derbe to Philippi
(Acts 16:1–5, 8–15)

**Sources:**

Barker, Kenneth L. and Kohlenberger III, John R., eds. *The Expositor's Bible Commentary – Abridged Edition: New Testament.* Grand Rapids, MI: Zondervan, 1994. 467-471.

Butler, Trent C., ed. "Derbe." *Holman Bible Dictionary.* Electronic Edition, Quickverse. Nashville, TN: Holman Bible Publishers, 1991.

Butler, Trent C., ed. "Philippi." *Holman Bible Dictionary.* Electronic Edition, Quickverse. Nashville, TN: Holman Bible Publishers, 1991.

Carson, D. A., R. T. France, J. A. Motyer, G. J. Wenham, Eds. *New Bible Commentary.* Downers Grove, IL: InterVarsity Press, 1994. 1090-1091.

Easton, M. G. "Philippi." *Easton's Bible Dictionary.* 1st ed. Oklahoma City, OK: Ellis Enterprises, 1993.

Elwell, Walter A. and Yarbrough, Robert W. *Encountering the New Testament: A Historical and Theological Survey.* Grand Rapids, MI: Baker Books, 1998. 238-242, 313.

Keener, Craig S. *The IVP Bible Background Commentary: New Testament.* Downers Grove, IL: InterVarsity Press, 1993. 366-369.

Thayer, Joseph. "dianoigō." *Thayer's Greek Definitions.* 3rd ed. Electronic Edition, Quickverse. El Cajon, CA: Institute for Creation Research, 1999.

Thayer, Joseph. "stereoō." *Thayer's Greek Definitions.* 3rd ed. Electronic Edition, Quickverse. El Cajon, CA: Institute for Creation Research, 1999.

Walvoord, John F. and Zuck, Roy B., eds. *The Bible Knowledge Commentary: An Exposition of the Scriptures.* Wheaton, IL: Victor Books, 1983. 398-399.

## COMMENTS / NOTES:

_____

_____

_____

_____

_____

_____

_____

_____

_____

_____

_____

_____

_____

_____

_____

_____

_____

_____

_____

_____

_____

_____

_____

_____

_____

_____

_____

_____

_____

# THESSALONICA, BEREA, AND ATHENS

**BIBLE BASIS:** Acts 17:1–4, 10–12, 22–25, 28

**BIBLE TRUTH:** Paul preached the Gospel with strong conviction in spite of opposition.

**MEMORY VERSE:** "For as I passed by, and beheld your devotions, I found an altar with this inscription, To The Unknown God. Whom therefore ye ignorantly worship, him declare I unto you" (Acts 17:23).

**LESSON AIM:** By the end of the lesson, we will: LEARN that, although Paul and Silas's message was accepted by some but not all, God received the glory; REFLECT on the effects of rejection in the lives of those who serve God; and SEEK out and use spiritual resources that support perseverance in the midst of rejection.

## LESSON SCRIPTURE

### ACTS 17:1–4, 10–12, 22–25, 28, KJV

1 Now when they had passed through Amphipolis and Apollonia, they came to Thessalonica, where was a synagogue of the Jews:

2 And Paul, as his manner was, went in unto them, and three sabbath days reasoned with them out of the scriptures,

3 Opening and alleging, that Christ must needs have suffered, and risen again from the dead; and that this Jesus, whom I preach unto you, is Christ.

4 And some of them believed, and consorted with Paul and Silas; and of the devout Greeks a great multitude, and of the chief women not a few.

10 And the brethren immediately sent away Paul and Silas by night unto Berea: who coming thither went into the synagogue of the Jews.

11 These were more noble than those in Thessalonica, in that they received the word with all readiness of mind, and searched the scriptures daily, whether those things were so.

12 Therefore many of them believed; also of honourable women which were Greeks, and of men, not a few.

22 Then Paul stood in the midst of Mars' hill, and said, Ye men of Athens, I perceive that in all things ye are too superstitious.

23 For as I passed by, and beheld your devotions, I found an altar with this inscription, To The Unknown God. Whom therefore ye ignorantly worship, him declare I unto you.

24 God that made the world and all things therein, seeing that he is Lord of heaven and earth, dwelleth not in temples made with hands;

25 Neither is worshipped with men's hands, as though he needed any thing, seeing he giveth to all life, and breath, and all things;

28 For in him we live, and move, and have our being; as certain also of your own poets have said, For we are also his offspring.

## LIFE NEED FOR TODAY'S LESSON

AIM: You will learn that some people expect verbal convictions while others reject them.

## INTRODUCTION

### Paul and Silas in Greece

Paul's second missionary journey took him and his companions Silas and Timothy into Greece. This is the first recorded time the Gospel reached Europe. His first stop was Philippi, a leading city of Macedonia and a Roman colony. There Paul preached to a riverside prayer meeting of women. Lydia, a wealthy woman who was a dealer of purple cloth, led the meeting. As Paul and Silas preached the Good News, the church in Philippi emerged from this all-woman prayer meeting.

Soon Paul and Silas encountered a local fortune teller who followed them through the marketplace. Knowing she was possessed by a demon, Paul commanded the evil spirit to leave her body. She was healed, but the men who gained money from her fortune-telling dragged Paul and Silas before the authorities. Consequently the two missionaries were thrown in jail. During the night while Paul and Silas were singing and praising God, an earthquake shook the jail. In the aftermath, the doors were opened and their bonds were unfastened. The jailer, thinking the prisoners had escaped, feared he would face punishment from the authorities. Instead Paul and Silas assured him they were still inside and preached to him the message of salvation. The jailer accepted. In a wise move, Paul claimed his Roman citizenship upon release in order to protect the church in Philippi from future harassment and persecution. Seeing that their church-planting job was done, Paul and Silas headed toward another significant city in Macedonia—Thessalonica.

## BIBLE LEARNING

AIM: You will learn that Paul's missionary journey took him to Philippi, Athens, Thessalonica, and Berea.

## I. INITIAL RECEPTION (Acts 17:1–4)

Paul and Silas arrived in Thessalonica to proclaim the Gospel. Their usual method was to start off proclaiming the Gospel in the synagogues, because Paul's fellow Jews would be a receptive audience to the message about their long-awaited Messiah. Paul's method included reasoning with them from the Scriptures in order to prove Jesus was the Christ. We can see from Paul's preaching in the synagogue that he used language and concepts familiar to his audience.

1 Now when they had passed through Amphipolis and Apollonia, they came to Thessalonica, where was a synagogue of the Jews: 2 And Paul, as his manner was, went in unto them, and three sabbath days reasoned with them out of the scriptures, 3 Opening and alleging, that Christ must needs have suffered, and risen again from the dead; and that this Jesus, whom I preach unto you, is Christ. 4 And some of them believed, and consorted with Paul and Silas; and of the devout Greeks a great multitude, and of the chief women not a few.

The Apostle Paul usually chose to preach the Gospel in large cities at key transportation hubs, so that the Good News could be spread beyond the places where he preached, a good example of strategizing for the most effective sharing of the Gospel. The Romans had built a road called the Egnatian Way, which stretched from the Adriatic Sea to the Hellespont. This very important road ran right through the city of Thessalonica, so once the message was planted, it could be carried west to the western shore of Greece or east to what is modern-day Turkey. Paul, Silas, and Timothy traveled from Philippi to Amphipolis to Apollonia to Thessalonica, a distance of about 100 miles, no easy stroll. No doubt Paul stopped overnight at both Amphipolis and Apollonia, but when morning came, he hurried on his way.

As always, if there was a synagogue in town, Paul began by preaching there, so that was the first place in Thessalonica that he went. He always had a heart to reach his own people first, even when his people rejected him and the Lord Jesus. Paul showed his listeners from Old Testament Scriptures that it was prophesied that the Messiah had to suffer and die, and then rise from the dead. The Greek word for alleging is *paratithemi* (**pa-ra-TEE-thay-me**) which literally means to place alongside; so we can see Paul setting prophecies alongside their fulfillment in Jesus.

Some of the Jews accepted this message, but there were a large number of Gentiles who had been attending the synagogue who turned to Jesus. Among the new believers were some from a variety of social positions, both men and women.

At first glance it looks like Paul was in Thessalonica for only three weeks, because our verses mention him preaching in the synagogue for only three Sabbaths, but when we look at **Philippians 4:15–16**, we see that the Philippian church sent offerings to Paul in Thessalonica twice, which would imply that Paul was there for a longer period. We also read in **1 Thessalonians 2:9** and **2 Thessalonians 3:7–10** that he supported himself, probably by tent-making (**Acts 18:3**), as he was waiting for the gifts from Philippi. And then we read in **1 Thessalonians 1:9** that most of the converts were steeped in idolatry, so obviously many who turned to Christ were

not from the synagogue. Then after three weeks of preaching in the synagogue, Paul began ministering in another part of the city. However, the leaders of the synagogue felt that Paul was stealing their converts, so they ran him out of town.

## SEARCH THE SCRIPTURES

### QUESTION 1
How many days did Paul speak with the Jews in the synagogue?

## II. INSPIRING RESEARCH (vv. 10–12)

Paul and Silas left Thessalonica in secret after certain jealous Jews gathered a crowd of wicked men in order to bring them before the authorities. On arriving in Berea, they did not deviate from their usual method but found a local synagogue. This audience was different: nobler, or more open-minded, than the people in Thessalonica. These Jews listened to the Gospel message with eagerness and searched the Scriptures to confirm whether it was true. Rabbis often praised those who listened attentively and searched the Scriptures. Greek philosophers also valued attentive, scrutinizing listeners.

The methods Paul and Silas used did not change, but they received different results in the two cities because they were preaching to different audiences. The Thessalonicans by and large received their message, despite some opposition. The Bereans eagerly listened and kept a tolerant and open mind. The Gospel challenged those in the synagogue at Berea in a positive way to research whether what Paul said was true. The apostles' rejection in Thessalonica did not discourage them from preaching the same message in Berea, and it produced great results.

**10 And the brethren immediately sent away Paul and Silas by night unto Berea: who**

coming thither went into the synagogue of the Jews. 11 These were more noble than those in Thessalonica, in that they received the word with all readiness of mind, and searched the scriptures daily, whether those things were so. 12 Therefore many of them believed; also of honourable women which were Greeks, and of men, not a few.

After the Jewish leaders of Thessalonica tried to have Paul executed, the believers in Thessalonica slipped Paul out of the city at night. Paul and Silas had a 45-mile hike to their next destination, the city of Berea. This was not such a prominent city, but at least the Jews here were not so prejudiced against the Gospel. The response of the Bereans in the synagogue was quite different from those in the Thessalonian synagogue. When Paul told them that the Messiah did not come the way they expected, they searched the Scriptures he was preaching from. The Greek word for searched is *anakrino* (**ah-na-KREE-no**), which is the word used for judicial investigations; in other words, they investigated, examined, and questioned critically. The Bereans were not content to accept at face value what Paul had to say, but daily checked his words with Old Testament Scripture. The question we can ask ourselves is, when we hear someone preach something we haven't heard before, what is our response? Are we like the Bereans—do we carefully check Scripture to see if this is the truth?

A number of prominent Greek women believed, as did devout Jews. This is probably underscored in both passages—in both Thessalonica and Berea, even wealthy men and women of other ethnicities received Jesus; anyone can receive the Gospel, no matter what socioeconomic class, no matter whether male or female.

## III. PROVOKING REFLECTION (vv. 22–25, 28)

The Jews from Thessalonica travel forty-five miles southwest to Berea and manage to incite the crowds. This forced Paul to escape by sea to Athens. While at Athens waiting for Silas and Timothy, Paul notices the city is full of idols. So he goes about his usual custom of proclaiming the Gospel in the synagogues and marketplace. A group of Epicurean and Stoic philosophers, confused by the claims of the Gospel message, invites him to the Areopagus, or Mars Hill, a place where the philosophers and intellectuals gathered to hear the newest and most innovative ideas.

Paul opens his speech with a compliment to the religious sensibilities of the people of Athens. This leads to him pointing out the inscription he noticed on an altar: "To the unknown God." He next uses this inscription and connects it to their ignorance of the God of the Bible. He is the unknown God who Paul will now proclaim to them. Paul goes on to use popular quotes from poets and philosophers of the day in order to convince them of the resurrection of Christ and their need to repent and believe in Him.

22 Then Paul stood in the midst of Mars' hill, and said, Ye men of Athens, I perceive that in all things ye are too superstitious. 23 For as I passed by, and beheld your devotions, I found an altar with this inscription, To The Unknown God. Whom therefore ye ignorantly worship, him declare I unto you. 24 God that made the world and all things therein, seeing that he is Lord of heaven and earth, dwelleth not in temples made with hands; 25 Neither is worshipped with men's hands, as though he needed any thing, seeing he giveth to all life, and breath, and all things;

The Thessalonian Jewish leaders who had chased Paul out of their city made the trip to Berea and did the same thing there, so the Berean believers escorted Paul out of their city and got him to Athens, presumably by boat, but Silas and Timothy stayed behind to continue teaching the new believers in Berea.

While Paul was waiting for Silas and Timothy to catch up with him in Athens, he was making use of every opportunity to share the Gospel. As was his custom, he used Old Jewish Scripture to convince Jews and Gentiles in the synagogue that Jesus is the Messiah God promised to send. He also hung out in the marketplace to discuss his faith with anyone who was interested. Athens was once the center of its own empire. Now that the Romans ruled, it had lost its political authority, but it was still known for its philosophers, including Plato, Socrates, and Aristotle from prior days. As a Jewish leader and an educated Roman citizen, Paul was a very educated and intelligent man. He was used to a teaching method that emphasized one-on-one debate, as well as the use of public debate.

This was a forum that met to decide matters of morals or religion. Paul began his defense of the Gospel by telling his listeners they were extremely *deisidaimon* (Gk. **day-cee-DIE-mone**), a word which has been translated as either religious or superstitious. This is vague in Greek and could be taken as complimentary (religious) or derogatory (superstitious). In this case, Paul would be complimenting them as being very devout in order to get their attention. As a further bridge into their thinking, he mentions the many altars to the unknown god that were scattered throughout the city. The Athenians had many, many idols, but just in case they missed one, there were a number of altars dedicated to the unknown god. This concept was introduced by a poet, Epiminedes. During a time when Athens was suffering from a plague, he

advised the rulers of Athens to sacrifice upon these altars and the plague was subsequently stopped. Because of this, Epiminedes was considered not only a poet but a prophet.

Paul said that he came to introduce them to the God they did not know—the God who created everything, the earth, the heavens, and everything on earth and in heaven. Not only is He the Creator, but also Ruler over everything. This God is too big to be contained in any earthly building. Even King Solomon, the builder of the first temple, acknowledged that God is too big to fit in any temple (**1 Kings 8:27**). And God is the one who sustains us; He does not need anything from us! In fact, our very life and breath are a gift from Him. Here, Paul states that what they have called the Unknown God out of ignorance is the true God. This is not an approval of their idolatry, but an affirmation of the partial truth that was revealed to them. This sets the stage for Paul to introduce them to the God who is the all-powerful, all-knowing, and all-present Creator of everything in existence.

**28 For in him we live, and move, and have our being; as certain also of your own poets have said, For we are also his offspring.**

In this verse, Paul quotes two Greek poets, both pagans. This surprises many modern Christians, who then wonder why these quotes are in our Bible. From this we can learn some valuable lessons on how to communicate the Gospel to unbelievers. If we can connect to our audience by quoting from sources our listeners are familiar with and that we can agree with, we will get their attention. For instance, if we quote a phrase from a popular rap song that has a kernel of truth in it, teens and young adults may be more willing to listen to us, especially if that quote can lead us to an explanation of the Gospel. In both of these quotes, Paul is showing something of the true nature of the one true God by affirming some truth found in Athenian culture.

Paul's first quote is that "in him we live, and move, and have our being." This quote is believed to be from Epiminedes in regards to Zeus, but Paul attributes it to Israel's God. The Stoic philosophers agreed with Paul on this point, as they believed in divine providence. In contrast, the Epicurean philosophers thought that the gods were too remote to be involved in the lives of human beings, but Paul is about to proclaim that God is as near as the air we breathe. It is only our sin that separates us from Him. Both we and the Greeks can look around at the things that God has made, including our own selves, and see that He is very near!

The second quote from the poet Aratus tells us that we are the offspring of God. The Stoic philosophers believed that there was a divine immanent principle in humanity, but Paul takes it a step further. For Paul, the phrase "we are his offspring" means that God created all humanity and we are ultimately responsible to Him. Later in the speech, Paul elaborates on this concept and concludes with a call to account for our actions and repent.

## SEARCH THE SCRIPTURES

### QUESTION 2
The men of _____ were thought to _____ (v. 22).

### QUESTION 3
The philosophers of Athens had an inscription on their altar that read _____ _____ (v. 23).

## BIBLE APPLICATION

AIM: You will see that believers are to evangelize in humility and faith in the work of the Holy Spirit.

Many times Christians are shown in the media as closed-minded and uneducated. Although this portrayal is far from the truth, many have bought into it. This results in many assumptions about those who share their Christian faith and the credibility of the Gospel message. Often our faith is insulted, and we face rejection from those around us. It is disheartening to feel as if the whole world believes the beliefs you hold are outdated and silly. In this lesson, we are encouraged to persevere in spite of rejection, knowing that God is the One who brings people to Him. This is what Paul did in order to see much fruit from his labors in preaching the Gospel.

## STUDENT'S RESPONSES

AIM: You will know that Christians can learn that the message of the Gospel may be rejected by those they hope will receive it.

Paul used the culture of Athens to create a bridge for the Gospel. Have the class create a list of contemporary cultural issues and religions. Next discuss the different ways the Gospel can address each issue. Encourage the class to seek common ground when sharing their faith in order to effectively communicate and minimize rejection for the wrong reasons.

## PRAYER

Jesus, we appreciate that we can share Your Word with those who do not know You and those who need to know You more. We rejoice in spreading the Good News of Christ! In the Name of Jesus, we pray. Amen.

## HOW TO SAY IT

| | |
|---|---|
| Agora. | ah-GOH-rah. |
| Amphipolis. | am-PHI-po-lis. |

| | |
|---|---|
| Apollonia. | ah-pol-**LON**-ee-ah. |
| Areopagus. | air-ee-**OP**-a-gus. |
| Berea. | ber-**EE**-ah. |
| Egnatian. | eg-**NA**-tian. |
| Thessalonica. | thes-sa-**LO**-nih-ka. |

## PREPARE FOR NEXT SUNDAY

Read **Acts 18:1–11, 18–21** and "Teaching God's Word."

## DAILY HOME BIBLE READINGS

### MONDAY
Creator God
(Deuteronomy 32:1–12)

### TUESDAY
Promises of God for All
(Genesis 9:8–17)

### WEDNESDAY
Blessing of God for All
(Genesis 12:1–4)

### THURSDAY
Majesty of God
(Psalm 8)

### FRIDAY
Goodness of God
(Psalm 33:13–22)

### SATURDAY
Reign of God
(Psalm 47)

### SUNDAY
Thessalonica, Berea, and Athens
(Acts 17:1–4, 10–12, 22–25, 28)

Bruce, F. F. *Commentary on the Book of the Acts: The New International Commentary on the New Testament.* Grand Rapids, MI: Wm. B. Eerdmans. Reprint, 1983.

Kisau, Paul Mumo. "Acts of the Apostles" from *Africa Bible Commentary.* General Editor: Tokunboh Adeyemo. Grand Rapids, MI: Zondervan, 2006.

Stott, John. *The Spirit of the Church and the World: The Message of Acts.* Downers Grove, IL: InterVarsity Press, 1990.

Toussaint, Stanley D. "Acts" from *The Bible Knowledge Commentary.* Editors: John F. Walvoord and Roy B. Zuck. Wheaton, IL: Victor Books, 1983.

## COMMENTS / NOTES:

_____

_____

_____

_____

_____

_____

_____

_____

_____

_____

_____

_____

_____

_____

_____

_____

_____

_____

_____

_____

_____

_____

_____

_____

_____

_____

_____

_____

_____

_____

**Sources:**
Barclay, William. *The Daily Study Bible: The Acts of the Apostles.* Philadelphia: The Westminster Press, 1955.

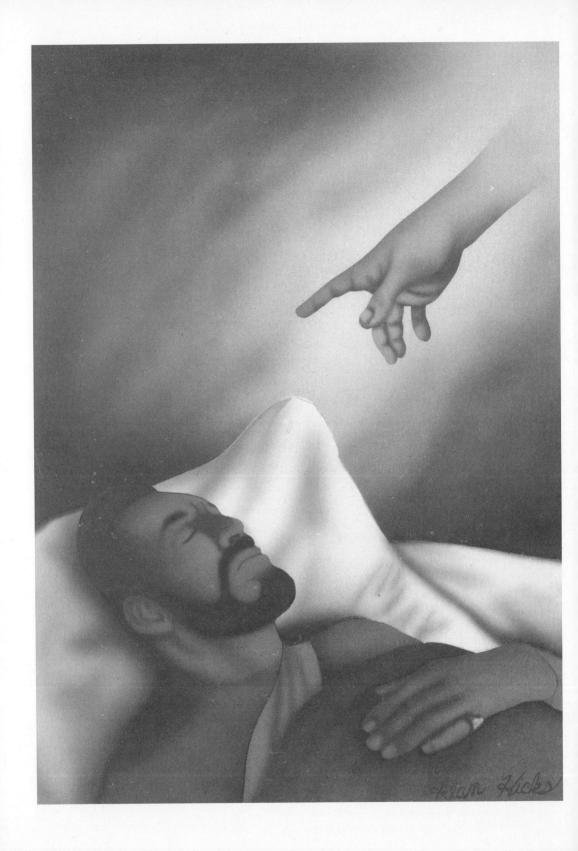

# TEACHING GOD'S WORD

**BIBLE BASIS:** ACTS 18:1–11, 18–21

**BIBLE TRUTH:** Luke writes of Paul's mission of proclaiming the Good News to Syria and Ephesus.

**MEMORY VERSE:** "Then spake the Lord to Paul in the night by a vision, Be not afraid, but speak, and hold not thy peace: For I am with thee, and no man shall set on thee to hurt thee: for I have much people in this city" (Acts 18:9–10).

**LESSON AIM:** By the end of the lesson, we will: REVIEW Paul's zeal for teaching the Gospel to the Gentiles; EXPLORE feelings after making a transition from a vocation, from rejection to praise; and PRAY for the success of those whom God has placed in a new situation.

## LESSON SCRIPTURE

### ACTS 18:1–11, 18–21, KJV

1 After these things Paul departed from Athens, and came to Corinth;

2 And found a certain Jew named Aquila, born in Pontus, lately come from Italy, with his wife Priscilla; (because that Claudius had commanded all Jews to depart from Rome:) and came unto them.

3 And because he was of the same craft, he abode with them, and wrought: for by their occupation they were tentmakers.

4 And he reasoned in the synagogue every sabbath, and persuaded the Jews and the Greeks.

5 And when Silas and Timotheus were come from Macedonia, Paul was pressed in the spirit, and testified to the Jews that Jesus was Christ.

6 And when they opposed themselves, and blasphemed, he shook his raiment, and said unto them, Your blood be upon your own heads; I am clean; from henceforth I will go unto the Gentiles.

7 And he departed thence, and entered into a certain man's house, named Justus, one that worshipped God, whose house joined hard to the synagogue.

8 And Crispus, the chief ruler of the synagogue, believed on the Lord with all his house; and many of the Corinthians hearing believed, and were baptized.

9 Then spake the Lord to Paul in the night by a vision, Be not afraid, but speak, and hold not thy peace:

10 For I am with thee, and no man shall set on thee to hurt thee: for I have much people in this city.

11 And he continued there a year and six months, teaching the word of God among them.

18 And Paul after this tarried there yet a good while, and then took his leave of the brethren, and sailed thence into Syria, and with him Priscilla and Aquila; having shorn his head in Cenchrea: for he had a vow.

19 And he came to Ephesus, and left them there: but he himself entered into the synagogue, and reasoned with the Jews.

**20** When they desired him to tarry longer time with them, he consented not;

**21** But bade them farewell, saying, I must by all means keep this feast that cometh in Jerusalem: but I will return again unto you, if God will. And he sailed from Ephesus.

## LIFE NEED FOR TODAY'S LESSON

**AIM: You will appreciate that people can be persistent when they really believe what they are doing and saying is the real thing.**

## INTRODUCTION
### Paul's Vision

In this lesson, we see Paul's focus on the mission and the calling he received from God. This focus has taken him further into the Gentile world and more specifically into the country of Greece. Prior to this, Paul and his companions intended to go into the region of Bithynia in the northernmost part of Asia Minor or modern-day Turkey. While on their way, Paul saw a vision of a man from Macedonia saying "Come over to Macedonia and help us." Taking this as the direction of the Holy Spirit, they set sail for the Grecian province of Macedonia. Immediately Paul and his companions Timothy and Silas began to preach in the cities of Thessalonica, Berea, and Athens. In each of these cities, Paul received a different response to the preaching of the Gospel. In Thessalonica, he was persecuted and run out of town. In Berea, many of his hearers listened and investigated the Scriptures to confirm Paul's message. Finally, in Athens, Paul encountered a mixed response—most of his audience rejected the Gospel, but a few requested him to come back again, while a few others believed.

Paul traveled southwest to the city of Corinth, which was a major commercial center and the leading city of Greece at the time. Although this was an ideal location to preach and plant a church among the Gentiles, Paul was afraid to preach in such a hostile environment (**1 Corinthians 2:3**). With encouragement from God, Paul continued to preach the Gospel and a vibrant church community was formed. Next, Paul would travel to Ephesus. There he would leave his coworkers Priscilla and Aquila and go on to Asia Minor and Syria to teach and encourage the churches he had founded on his first missionary journey with Barnabas. Soon he would return to Ephesus and continue the ministry of the Word.

## BIBLE LEARNING

**AIM: You will know that after experiencing a vision, Paul, Timothy, and Silas traveled together to various cities to preach.**

## I. OCCUPIED WITH THE WORD (Acts 18:1–5)

Paul lands in Corinth, and we get a more in-depth view of his usual ministry methods and lifestyle. He is alone in a new city and meets a Jewish couple, Priscilla and Aquila. They are recent immigrants to Corinth after the emperor Claudius banished all Jews from Rome. Since they shared the common occupation of tentmaking, Paul decided to stay and work with them. This was very strategic on Paul's part; his character would be on display as he lived in their home and worked in their workshop, presenting many opportunities to preach the Gospel and share his faith. Luke, the writer of Acts, also records that every Sabbath, Paul "reasoned in the synagogue" and attempted to "persuade Jews and Greeks" (**v. 4**). In the same way, our character is always on display no matter what occupation we have, and God has presented opportunities for us to share His Word no matter where we are.

During this time, Timothy and Silas come down from Macedonia to join Paul in preaching the

Gospel. It says that as soon as they came, Paul was "pressed in the spirit" (v. 5). This phrase means that he was occupied solely with one thing: preaching the Word. The ESV and other contemporary translations read "with the word" rather than "with the spirit" because the oldest Greek manuscripts say word. Either way, the text is telling us that Paul is focused on the Gospel. As he made tents with Priscilla and Aquila, he was also focused on sharing the Gospel and teaching those around him the Word of God. Even without help from his companions, he went to the synagogue every Sabbath to convince those in attendance of the truth about Jesus. The difference between then and after Timothy and Silas arrived in Corinth is he can now devote himself exclusively to the task of preaching. Whether we are in full-time ministry or work in a non-church-related occupation, the Lord wants us to be occupied with His Word and how we can share it with others.

## Acts 18:1–4, 18–21, 24–28

1 After these things Paul departed from Athens, and came to Corinth; 2 And found a certain Jew named Aquila, born in Pontus, lately come from Italy, with his wife Priscilla; (because that Claudius had commanded all Jews to depart from Rome:) and came unto them. 3 And because he was of the same craft, he abode with them, and wrought: for by their occupation they were tentmakers. 4 And he reasoned in the synagogue every sabbath, and persuaded the Jews and the Greeks. 5 And when Silas and Timotheus were come from Macedonia, Paul was pressed in the spirit, and testified to the Jews that Jesus was Christ.

In the beginning of the chapter, we read that Paul left Athens for the city of Corinth (Gk. *Korinthos,* **KOR-een-thoce**), which was named for a grape that was grown abundantly in the area. Located about 50 miles west of Athens, Corinth was the political and economic bedrock of Greece. Its infamy, however, was its reputation of sexual immorality. There were a dozen temples of worship specializing in lewd and lascivious sexual accommodations. Paul's missionary journey preaching the Gospel seems to have taken him from one challenging place of ministry to another.

When Paul arrived in Corinth, he again sought out Christian community and co-laborers in Christ. While ministering in Athens alone, Paul had no doubt learned the hard way that companionship in ministry affords increased spiritual and physical strength. Paul's first order of business was to find believers. He soon meets Aquila, along with his wife Priscilla. Eventually, this couple became missionary partners with Paul near the end of this two-year journey. Here at their introduction, they are described as residents of Italy, but it is made clear that they were Jewish by birth and religion. The Roman emperor Claudius had issued an edict banishing Jews from the capital. Other historical sources say he did this because Jews were causing unrest at the instigation of Christ. Likely what happened was that the traditional Jews and Jewish Christians came into religious conflict, and not recognizing a difference between the religions, Claudius banished all the "Jews" who were causing problems. It was from this edict of religious persecution that the Gospel spread wherever converts and disciples dispersed.

Priscilla and Aquila modeled for believers an egalitarian paradigm for partnership in vocation and ministry. Emphasizing community and companionship rather than gender competitiveness, they complemented each other as tentmakers and teachers. Priscilla and Aquila opened their homes in Ephesus (**1 Corinthians 16:19**) and Rome (**Romans 16:3–5**) to found house churches. Within this partnership of marriage and ministry, Paul found companionship and community among Christians, because he was also a tent-maker (Gk. *skenopoios,* **skay-no-poy-OSE**), or one who fashions tents from leather or goat hair. The term was also used in general for a leatherworker.

Together, the three of them took pride in their craft and enjoyed Christian fellowship as they made tents to house the very Roman soldiers who were their adversaries. This model of bi-vocational ministry is useful even today as it can give someone an avenue to preach the Gospel to those outside the church. It also is helpful as a means of changing the reputation of the clergy as those who are only interested in financial gain.

Paul worked throughout the week, but every Sabbath, he headed to the synagogue. Ever diligent to the cause of the Gospel, he "reasoned" (Gk. *dialegomai,* **dee-ah-LEH-go-my**), or engaged in lively, thoughtful, passionate discussion, continually and repeatedly with the Jews and Greeks regarding the Christ. Paul's goal was to persuade (Gk. *peitho,* **PAY-tho**), that is, to induce others to believe, usually by words or other fair means. Paul taught the Gospel to convert both Jews well-versed in Jewish Scripture and tradition and God-fearing Greeks well-versed in philosophy but who had not converted to Judaism.

## SEARCH THE SCRIPTURES

### QUESTION 1
Explain why Paul stayed with Aquila and his wife Priscilla.

## II. ENCOURAGED BY THE LORD (vv. 6–11)

The response from the Jews in the synagogue was hostility and opposition. They formed an organized resistance against Paul and insulted him. This caused Paul to shake his clothes and give a disclaimer of responsibility for their souls. They have heard the Word and now will be accountable to it. This is definitely the course of action we need to take when confronted with those who refuse to hear the Gospel. Next, Paul goes to the house of Titius Justus, a Gentile God-fearer who lived next door to the synagogue. The results of Paul's ministry are remarkable in that the synagogue ruler Crispus believed the Gospel along with his entire household. Additionally, Luke records that many people believed and were baptized.

In spite of this activity, it seems Paul needed some extra encouragement from the Lord. It may have been because of the opposition of the Jews or the immorality that filled Corinth. In any case, he receives a vision at night from the Lord. In the vision, Paul hears the Lord encourage him not to be afraid and to continue to preach the Gospel. God is with him, no one is going to harm him, and the Lord has many people in the city ready to respond to the message of salvation. Sometimes God is working with us in circumstances that may not seem favorable, but it is our job to continue to preach the Word. There are people who need to hear the message, and God has already prepared their hearts.

6 And when they opposed themselves, and blasphemed, he shook his raiment, and said unto them, Your blood be upon your own heads; I am clean; from henceforth I will go unto the Gentiles. 9 Then spake the Lord to Paul in the night by a vision, Be not afraid, but speak, and hold not thy peace: 10 For I am with thee, and no man shall set on thee to hurt thee: for I have much people in this city. 7 And he departed thence, and entered into a certain man's house, named Justus, one that worshipped God, whose house joined hard to the synagogue. 8 And Crispus, the chief ruler of the synagogue, believed on the Lord with all his house; and many of the Corinthians hearing believed, and were

baptized. **11 And he continued there a year and six months, teaching the word of God among them.**

Paul was making tents and preaching the Gospel whenever he had the opportunity. Once Silas and Timothy arrived, he was "pressed (Gk. *sunecho*, **soon-EK-oh**) in spirit." The word is used for being physically held or confined as a prisoner, and for besieging a city. In this context, it is intended metaphorically to mean the narrowing of Paul's focus. Now he is devoted exclusively to preaching the Gospel and testifying that "Jesus was Christ." The King James Version of the passage states that the Jews' reaction to Paul is that they "opposed themselves." In the active voice, it means to "arrange in battle array face to face." In the middle voice, it is translated "opposed yourself" against someone or to set yourself in opposition against someone. Although the militaristic denotation is still in mind in the middle and passive voice, a better rendering of the text is "resisted" (Gk. *antitasso*, **an-tee-TAHS-so**). Paul's response was to shake out his garment. This act was a disclaimer of any responsibility. Paul took his preaching of the Gospel seriously, in the same vein as the prophet Ezekiel (**Ezekiel 3:18, 33:4, 8**). He was accountable for preaching the message but not whether that message was obeyed. This signals his focus in preaching shifting to the Gentiles of Corinth.

Next Paul finds himself preaching and teaching in the house of Justus. This man is described as a God-fearer whose house was right next to the synagogue. Through Paul's activity during this time, Crispus, the leader of the synagogue, came to believe in the Lord along with his household. Crispus is a Latin name, so he may have been a Roman citizen. Luke might point this out to paint the Christian faith as favorable to the empire. There were also many others in Corinth who believed and became members of the newly emerging church in the city. This is the beginning of the rift between the Jewish and Christian communities. Until now, the disciples have been regarded as a Jewish sect. Soon they will be considered a different religion, with the destruction of Jerusalem in AD 70 sealing this separation.

Paul receives a vision at night. The Lord speaks to him and encourages him to stop being afraid. We know Paul experienced persecution in other Greek cities and from the Jews, especially when preaching in Thessalonica and Berea. He already experienced hostility from the Jews in the synagogue and may have anticipated another even more life-threatening incident. God encourages him to "hold not thy peace." This verb is imperative, which makes God's words to Paul a command to continue habitually doing something. In other words, he must go on speaking.

## SEARCH THE SCRIPTURES

### QUESTION 2
Who is Crispus?

## III. COMPELLED TO RETURN (vv. 18–21)

Paul stayed in Corinth for about a year and six months. The opposition of the Jews continued until it finally climaxed with a trial before the Roman proconsul Gallio. Gallio sees the trial as a matter of Jewish customs and admonishes them to take care of it themselves. Luke mentions this trial in order to show Christianity as a non-threat to the Roman Empire; it was a Jewish affair, not a subversive cult.

After this, Paul continues a few days in Corinth after the trial and then heads off for Syria. When they reach Cenchreae, a city on the coast, Paul shaves his head to fulfill a vow. This was in fulfillment of the Nazarite vow (**Numbers 6:1–21**), which indicated that

Paul had consecrated himself to the Lord for a period of time. The vow included avoiding alcoholic drinks and letting one's hair grow, so shaving his head indicates his period of consecration is complete. Accompanied by Priscilla and Aquila, he stops at Ephesus, where he goes into the synagogue and begins to reason with the Jews. This seems to be a test or experiment to investigate the kind of reception the Gospel would obtain in the city. The Jews in the synagogue at Ephesus seem to be curious and hungry for the Gospel as they ask him to stay for a longer period of time. Paul declines their request; he must go on to encourage and teach the churches he formed in Asia Minor. He lets them know his desire is to return, but it is ultimately up to God. Paul sets sail from Ephesus because he also believes in strengthening the churches he left behind. It is not an either/or thing with Paul. His goal, as well as ours, is to see people built up in Christ and this includes encouraging and teaching God's Word to those who are already followers of Christ. He does this in order for them to mature in the faith.

**18 And Paul after this tarried there yet a good while, and then took his leave of the brethren, and sailed thence into Syria, and with him Priscilla and Aquila; having shorn his head in Cenchrea: for he had a vow. 19 And he came to Ephesus, and left them there: but he himself entered into the synagogue, and reasoned with the Jews. 20 When they desired him to tarry longer time with them, he consented not; 21 But bade them farewell, saying, I must by all means keep this feast that cometh in Jerusalem: but I will return again unto you, if God will.**

While teaching many of those gathering in the synagogue weekly, Paul "tarried" (Gk. *prosmeno*, **pros-MEN-oh**), meaning "to continue" or "to remain with" them for an unspecified length of time, but for what is understood to be a considerable number of days. Paul stayed put, preaching and teaching among them, even after a plot to kill him had failed (**18:12–17**). Because the people were receptive, the Word effectively convinced them that Jesus is the Christ. Note that in the previous verse, those gathered were called Jews and Greeks. After Paul's effective and persuasive ministry to them, he now calls them "brethren" (Gk. *adelphos*, **ah-del-FOSE**), which can refer to a brother by birth, national origin, or friendship. However within the Christian context, in its plural form of *adelphoi* (Gk. **ah-del-FOY**), the term became all-inclusive to refer to all who believed, whether Jew or Greek, slave or free.

The "vow" (Gk. *euche*, **ew-KHAY**) that Paul made earlier was most likely a 7-day Nazarite vow when he did not shave or drink wine (cf. **Acts 21:23**). Shaving his head was simply an outward Jewish expression of his inward sincerity when this period of consecration had ended.

The Roman city Ephesus was located on the coast of what is today western Turkey, about 55 miles north from Miletus—the place from which Paul would call the elders of the church (**Acts 20:17**). While in port at Ephesus, Paul left his companions, Priscilla and Aquila, and went directly to the synagogue to again debate with the Jewish religious and philosophical leaders assembled there. Paul was ever ready and seeking to persuade, convince, debate, and prove that Jesus Christ is the Messiah to all who would listen. The Greek word *sunagoge* (**soo-naw-go-GAY**) is a building and also the formal assembly of Jews who gathered in such a building to pray, read, and discuss Scripture. Synagogue services were held weekly on the Sabbath and on special feast days. The synagogue could also be used for trials. Every town with at least ten Jewish males free to practice their religion could have a synagogue.

Paul's teaching was so efficacious that Jewish religious leaders asked him to tarry (Gk. *meno*, **MEH-no**), or stay with them, a while longer. Even though Paul hastened from the port of Ephesus to meet with those in the synagogue, he was compelled by the Holy Spirit to decline their persistence that he extend his stay. The text says he did not consent (Gk. *epineuo*, **eh-pee-NEW-oh**). The original word means to nod and implies assent. Here, Paul demonstrates that his calling and ministry is to do God's will, not man's desire. The good work to be done among these new believers paled in comparison to the ministry before Paul as he journeyed to Jerusalem for the Feast of the Passover.

## SEARCH THE SCRIPTURES

### QUESTION 3
Where did Paul journey to after he left Ephesus for what feast?

## BIBLE APPLICATION

**AIM: You will know that God can place us in a situation where our knowledge and skills are embraced so that He is glorified.**

Preaching the Gospel is often seen as annoying and offensive, or as someone imposing their beliefs on another. Far from it. As Paul preached and taught, he appealed to the reason of his audience while also acknowledging their freedom of choice and personal responsibility. He was a man with a single-minded focus because he believed God was at work in the hearts of those around him. This ought to encourage us to pray and ask God to give us eyes to see Him at work and assurance that He is with us to equip and protect us. Whether at work or a softball game, we may be presented with opportunities to share our faith. We can also pray for others in new and challenging situations. We can pray for them to keep their eyes open and their hearts focused on the one thing that matters: the Good News of Jesus Christ.

## STUDENT'S RESPONSES

**AIM: You will know that believers can pray and praise God for sustaining their work or vocations.**

Sometimes opportunities to share our faith can be right under our noses. There may be someone at your work or in your neighborhood whom God may be highlighting to you. One of the best contexts to get to know someone and share our lives is mealtime. Make a plan to sit down in the coming week and eat with at least three people who do not know Christ. Pray for an opportunity to share the Gospel and watch what God does.

## PRAYER

Thank You for sending missionaries to spread the Good News of Christ. Thank You for missionaries who share the Good News in the local community and globally. In the Name of Jesus, we pray. Amen.

## HOW TO SAY IT

| | |
|---|---|
| Pontus. | **PAHN**-tis. |
| Aquila. | ah-**KWI**-luh. |
| Priscilla. | pris-**SI**-luh. |

## PREPARE FOR NEXT SUNDAY

Read **Exodus 20:8–11, 31:12–16** and "The Lord's Day."

**DAILY HOME BIBLE READINGS**

**MONDAY**
Learning from God
(Psalm 25:8–12, 20–21)

**TUESDAY**
Living with God
(Psalm 27:4–5, 8–9, 11–14)

**WEDNESDAY**
Wisdom from God
(Proverbs 16:19–24)

**THURSDAY**
Commissioned to Teach
(Matthew 28:16–20)

**FRIDAY**
Teach Me Your Ways
(Exodus 33:12–18)

**SATURDAY**
Apollos Grows in Ministry
(Acts 18:24–28)

**SUNDAY**
Teaching God's Word
(Acts 18:1–11, 18–21)

**Sources:**
Keener, Craig S. *IVP Bible Background Commentary*. Downers Grove, IL: InterVarsity Press, 1993.
Carson, D.A., France, R.T., Motyer, J.A., Wenham, J.G. *New Bible Commentary*. Downers Grove, IL: InterVarsity Press, 1993.
Polhill, John B. Acts. *New American Commentary: An Exegetical and Theological Exposition of Holy Scripture*. Nashville: B&H Publishing, 1992.

## COMMENTS / NOTES:

# NOTES

# NOTES

# NOTES

# NOTES

# NOTES

# NOTES

# NOTES

# NOTES

# NOTES

# NOTES

# NOTES

# NOTES

# NOTES

# NOTES

# NOTES

# NOTES

# NOTES

# NOTES

## The Symbol of the Church Of God In Christ

The Symbol of the Church Of God In Christ is an outgrowth of the Presiding Bishop's Coat of Arms, which has become quite familiar to the Church. The design of the Official Seal of the Church was created in 1973 and adopted in the General Assembly in 1981 (July Session).

The obvious GARNERED WHEAT in the center of the seal represents all of the people of the Church Of God In Christ, Inc. The ROPE of wheat that holds the shaft together represents the Founding Father of the Church, Bishop Charles Harrison Mason, who, at the call of the Lord, banded us together as a Brotherhood of Churches in the First Pentecostal General Assembly of the Church, in 1907.

The date in the seal has a two-fold purpose: first, to tell us that Bishop Mason received the baptism of the Holy Ghost in March 1907 and, second, to tell us that it was because of this outpouring that Bishop Mason was compelled to call us together in February of 1907 to organize the Church Of God In Christ.

The RAIN in the background represents the Latter Rain, or the End-time Revivals, which brought about the emergence of our Church along with other Pentecostal Holiness Bodies in the same era. The rain also serves as a challenge to the Church to keep Christ in the center of our worship and service, so that He may continue to use the Church Of God In Christ as one of the vehicles of Pentecostal Revival before the return of the Lord.

This information was reprinted from the book *So You Want to KNOW YOUR CHURCH* by Alferd Z. Hall, Jr.

## COGIC AFFIRMATION OF FAITH

We believe the Bible to be the inspired and only infallible written Word of God.

We believe that there is One God, eternally existent in three Persons: God the Father, God the Son, and God the Holy Spirit.

We believe in the Blessed Hope, which is the rapture of the Church of God, which is in Christ at His return.

We believe that the only means of being cleansed from sin is through repentance and faith in the precious Blood of Jesus Christ.

We believe that regeneration by the Holy Ghost is absolutely essential for personal salvation.

We believe that the redemptive work of Christ on the Cross provides healing for the human body in answer to believing in prayer.

We believe that the baptism in the Holy Ghost, according to Acts 2:4, is given to believers who ask for it.

We believe in the sanctifying power of the Holy Spirit, by whose indwelling the Christian is enabled to live a Holy and separated life in this present world. Amen.

## The Doctrines of the Church Of God In Christ

### THE BIBLE

We believe that the Bible is the Word of God and contains one harmonious and sufficiently complete system of doctrine. We believe in the full inspiration of the Word of God. We hold the Word of God to be the only authority in all matters and assert that no doctrine can be true or essential if it does not find a place in this Word.

### THE FATHER

We believe in God, the Father Almighty, the Author and Creator of all things. The Old Testament reveals God in diverse manners, by manifesting His nature, character, and dominions. The Gospels in the New Testament give us knowledge of God the "Father" or "My Father," showing the relationship of God to Jesus as Father, or representing Him as the Father in the Godhead, and Jesus himself that Son (St. John 15:8, 14:20). Jesus also gives God the distinction of "Fatherhood" to all believers when He explains God in the light of "Your Father in Heaven" (St. Matthew 6:8).

### THE SON

We believe that Jesus Christ is the Son of God, the second person in the Godhead of the Trinity or Triune Godhead. We believe that Jesus was and is eternal in His person and nature as the Son of God who was with God in the beginning of creation (St. John 1:1). We believe that Jesus Christ was born of a virgin called Mary according to the Scripture (St. Matthew 1:18), thus giving rise to our fundamental belief in the Virgin Birth and to all of the miraculous events surrounding the phenomenon (St. Matthew 1:18–25). We believe that Jesus Christ became the "suffering servant" to man; this suffering servant came seeking to redeem man from sin and to reconcile him to God, his Father (Romans 5:10). We believe that Jesus Christ is standing now as mediator between God and man (I Timothy 2:5).

## THE HOLY GHOST

We believe the Holy Ghost or Holy Spirit is the third person of the Trinity; proceeds from the Father and the Son; is of the same substance, equal to power and glory; and is together with the Father and the Son, to be believed in, obeyed, and worshiped. The Holy Ghost is a gift bestowed upon the believer for the purpose of equipping and empowering the believer, making him or her a more effective witness for service in the world. He teaches and guides one into all truth (John 16:13; Acts 1:8, 8:39).

## THE BAPTISM OF THE HOLY GHOST

We believe that the Baptism of the Holy Ghost is an experience subsequent to conversion and sanctification and that tongue-speaking is the consequence of the baptism in the Holy Ghost with the manifestations of the fruit of the spirit (Galatians 5:22–23; Acts 10:46, 19:1–6). We believe that we are not baptized with the Holy Ghost in order to be saved (Acts 19:1–6; John 3:5). When one receives a baptismal Holy Ghost experience, we believe one will speak with a tongue unknown to oneself according to the sovereign will of Christ. To be filled with the Spirit means to be Spirit controlled as expressed by Paul in Ephesians 5:18,19. Since the charismatic demonstrations were necessary to help the early church to be successful in implementing the command of Christ, we, therefore, believe that a Holy Ghost experience is mandatory for all believers today.

## MAN

We believe that humankind was created holy by God, composed of body, soul, and spirit. We believe that humankind, by nature, is sinful and unholy. Being born in sin, a person needs to be born again, sanctified and cleansed from all sins by the blood of Jesus. We believe that one is saved by confessing and forsaking one's sins, and believing on the Lord Jesus Christ, and that having become a child of God, by being born again and adopted into the family of God, one may, and should, claim the inheritance of the sons of God, namely the baptism of the Holy Ghost.

## SIN

Sin, the Bible teaches, began in the angelic world (Ezekiel 28:11–19; Isaiah 14:12–20) and is transmitted into the blood of the human race through disobedience and deception motivated by unbelief (I Timothy 2:14). Adam's sin, committed by eating of the forbidden fruit from the tree of knowledge of good and evil, carried with it permanent pollution or depraved human nature to all his descendants. This is called "original sin." Sin can now be defined as a volitional transgression against God and a lack of conformity to the will of God. We, therefore, conclude that humankind by nature is sinful and has fallen from a glorious and righteous state from which we were created, and has become unrighteous and unholy. We therefore, must be restored to the state of holiness from which we have fallen by being born again (St. John 3:7).

## SALVATION

Salvation deals with the application of the work of redemption to the sinner with restoration to divine favor and communion with God. This redemptive operation of the Holy Ghost upon sinners is brought about by repentance toward God and faith toward our Lord Jesus Christ which brings conversion, faith, justification, regeneration, sanctification, and the baptism of the Holy Ghost. Repentance is the work of God, which results in a change of mind in respect to a person's relationship to God (St. Matthew 3:1–2, 4:17; Acts 20:21). Faith is a certain conviction wrought in the heart by the Holy Spirit, as to the truth of the Gospel and a heart trust in the promises of God in Christ (Romans 1:17, 3:28; St. Matthew 9:22; Acts 26:18). Conversion is that act of God whereby He causes the regenerated sinner, in one's conscious life, to turn to Him in repentance and faith (II Kings 5:15; II Chronicles 33:12,13; St. Luke 19:8,9; Acts 8:30). Regeneration is the act of God by which the principle of the new life is implanted in humankind, the governing disposition of soul is made holy, and the first holy exercise of this new disposition is secured. Sanctification is that gracious and continuous operation of the Holy Ghost, by which He delivers the justified sinner from the pollution of sin, renews a person's whole nature in the image of God, and enables one to perform good works (Romans 6:4, 5:6; Colossians 2:12, 3:1).

## ANGELS

The Bible uses the term "angel" (a heavenly body) clearly and primarily to denote messengers or ambassadors of God with such Scripture references as Revelations 4:5, which indicates their duty in heaven to praise God (Psalm 103:20), to do God's will (St. Matthew 18:10), and to behold His face. But since heaven must come down to earth, they also have a mission to earth. The Bible indicates that they accompanied God in the Creation, and also that they will accompany Christ in His return in Glory.

## DEMONS

Demons denote unclean or evil spirits; they are sometimes called devils or demonic beings. They are evil spirits, belonging to the unseen or spiritual realm, embodied in human beings. The Old Testament refers to the prince of demons, sometimes called Satan (adversary) or Devil, as having power and wisdom, taking the habitation of other forms such as the serpent (Genesis 3:1). The New Testament speaks of the Devil as Tempter (St. Matthew 4:3), and it goes on to tell the works of Satan, the Devil, and demons as combating righteousness and good in any form, proving to be an adversary to the saints. Their chief power is exercised to destroy the mission of Jesus Christ. It can well be said that the Christian Church believes in demons, Satan, and devils. We believe in their power and purpose. We believe they can be subdued and conquered as in the commandment to the believer by Jesus. "In my name they shall cast out Satan and the work of the Devil and to resist him and then he will flee (WITHDRAW) from you" (St. Mark 16:17).

## THE CHURCH

The Church forms a spiritual unity of which Christ is the divine head. It is animated by one Spirit, the Spirit of Christ. It professes one faith, shares one hope, and serves one King. It is the citadel of the truth and God's agency for communicating to believers all spiritual blessings. The Church then is the object of our faith rather than of knowledge. The name of our Church, "CHURCH OF GOD IN CHRIST," is supported by I Thessalonians 2:14 and other passages in the Pauline Epistles. The word "CHURCH" or "EKKLESIA" was first applied to the Christian society by Jesus Christ in St. Matthew 16:18, the occasion being that of His benediction of Peter at Caesarea Philippi.

## THE SECOND COMING OF CHRIST

We believe in the second coming of Christ; that He shall come from heaven to earth, personally, bodily, visibly (Acts 1:11; Titus 2:11–13; St. Matthew 16:27, 24:30, 25:30; Luke 21:27; John 1:14, 17; Titus 2:11); and that the Church, the bride, will be caught up to meet Him in the air (I Thessalonians 4:16–17). We admonish all who have this hope to purify themselves as He is pure.

## DIVINE HEALING

The Church Of God In Christ believes in and practices Divine Healing. It is a commandment of Jesus to the Apostles (St. Mark 16:18). Jesus affirms His teachings on healing by explaining to His disciples, who were to be Apostles, that healing the afflicted is by faith (St. Luke 9:40–41). Therefore, we believe that healing by faith in God has scriptural support and ordained authority. St. James's writings in his epistle encourage Elders to pray for the sick, lay hands upon them and to anoint them with oil, and state that prayers with faith shall heal the sick and the Lord shall raise them up. Healing is still practiced widely and frequently in the Church Of God In Christ, and testimonies of healing in our Church testify to this fact.

## MIRACLES

The Church Of God In Christ believes that miracles occur to convince people that the Bible is God's Word. A miracle can be defined as an extraordinary visible act of divine power, wrought by the efficient agency of the will of God, which has as its final cause the vindication of the righteousness of God's Word. We believe that the works of God, which were performed during the beginnings of Christianity, do and will occur even today where God is preached, faith in Christ is exercised, the Holy Ghost is active, and the Gospel is promulgated in the truth (Acts 5:15, 6:8, 9:40; Luke 4:36, 7:14, 15, 5:5, 6; St. Mark 14:15).

## THE ORDINANCES OF THE CHURCH

It is generally admitted that for an ordinance to be valid, it must have been instituted by Christ. When we speak of ordinances of the church, we are speaking of those instituted by Christ, in which by sensible signs the grace of God in Christ and the benefits of the covenant of grace are represented, sealed, and applied to believers, and these in turn give expression to their faith and allegiance to God. The Church Of God In Christ recognizes three ordinances as having been instituted by Christ himself and, therefore, are binding upon the church practice.

## THE LORD'S SUPPER (HOLY COMMUNION)

The Lord's Supper symbolizes the Lord's death and suffering for the benefit and in the place of His people. It also symbolizes the believer's participation in the crucified Christ. It represents not only the death of Christ as the object of faith, which unites the believers to Christ, but also the effect of this act as the giving of life, strength, and joy to the soul. The communicant by faith enters into a special spiritual union of one's soul with the glorified Christ.

## FOOT WASHING

Foot washing is practiced and recognized as an ordinance in our Church because Christ, by His example, showed that humility characterized greatness in the kingdom of God, and that service rendered to others gave evidence that humility, motivated by love, exists. These services are held subsequent to the Lord's Supper; however, its regularity is left to the discretion of the pastor in charge.

## WATER BAPTISM

We believe that Water Baptism is necessary as instructed by Christ in St. John 3:5, "UNLESS MAN BE BORN AGAIN OF WATER AND OF THE SPIRIT..."

However, we do not believe that water baptism alone is a means of salvation, but is an outward demonstration that one has already had a conversion experience and has accepted Christ as his personal Savior. As Pentecostals, we practice immersion in preference to sprinkling because immersion corresponds more closely to the death, burial, and resurrection of our Lord (Colossians 2:12). It also symbolizes regeneration and purification more than any other mode. Therefore, we practice immersion as our mode of baptism. We believe that we should use the Baptismal Formula given to us by Christ for all "...IN THE NAME OF THE FATHER, AND OF THE SON, AND OF THE HOLY GHOST..." (Matthew 28:19).

# Suggested Order of Service

1. Call to order.

2. Singing.

3. Prayer.

4. Responsive reading:

**Supt.:** Behold, how good and how pleasant it is for brethren to dwell together in unity!
*Psalm 133:1*

**School:** And let the peace of God rule in your hearts, to the which also ye are called in one body; and be ye thankful.
*Colossians 3:15*

**Supt.:** Blessed are they that dwell in thy house: they will be still praising thee.
*Psalm 84:4*

**School:** Praise ye the LORD. I will praise the LORD with my whole heart, in the assembly of the upright, and in the congregation.
*Psalm 111:1*

**Supt.:** And the LORD said unto him, I have heard thy prayer and thy supplication, that thou hast made before me: I have hallowed this house, which thou hast built, to put my name there for ever; and mine eyes and mine heart shall be there perpetually.
*1 Kings 9:3*

**School:** Ye shall keep my sabbaths, and reverence my sanctuary: I am the LORD.
*Leviticus 19:30*

**Supt.:** And I say also unto thee, That thou art Peter, and upon this rock I will build my church; and the gates of hell shall not prevail against it.
*Matthew 16:18*

**School:** My soul longeth, yea, even fainteth for the courts of the LORD: my heart and my flesh crieth out for the living God.
*Psalm 84:2*

**Supt.:** And other sheep I have, which are not of this fold: them also I must bring, and they shall hear my voice; and there shall be one fold, and one shepherd.
*John 10:16*

**School:** But if I tarry long, that thou mayest know how thou oughtest to behave thyself in the house of God, which is the church of the living God, the pillar and ground of the truth.
*1 Timothy 3:15*

**All:** Lift up your hands in the sanctuary, and bless the LORD.
*Psalm 134:2*

5. Singing.

6. Reading lesson by school and superintendent.

7. Classes assemble for lesson study.

8. Sunday School offering.

9. Five-minute warning bell.

10. Closing bell.

11. Brief lesson review by pastor or superintendent.

12. Secretary's report.

13. Announcements.

14. Dismissal.